Knowing the Self

Knowing the Self

Attachment and Therapeutic Alliance for Mental Health Professionals

YUSMARHAINI YUSOF

BLOOMSBURY ACADEMIC
LONDON • NEW YORK • OXFORD • NEW DELHI • SYDNEY

BLOOMSBURY ACADEMIC
Bloomsbury Publishing Plc
50 Bedford Square, London, WC1B 3DP, UK
1385 Broadway, New York, NY 10018, USA
29 Earlsfort Terrace, Dublin 2, Ireland

BLOOMSBURY, BLOOMSBURY ACADEMIC and the Diana logo are
trademarks of Bloomsbury Publishing Plc

First published 2019 by RED GLOBE PRESS
Reprinted by Bloomsbury Academic, 2023

For legal purposes the Acknowledgements on p. ix constitute
an extension of this copyright page.

A catalogue record for this book is available from the British Library.

A catalog record for this book is available from the Library of Congress.

ISBN: PB: 978-1-352-00732-9
ePDF: 978-1-352-00733-6
ePub: 978-1-350-30577-9

Table of Contents

List of Exercises

List of Figures, Tables and Case Studies

Figure

Table

Case Studies

Acknowledgements

This book is made possible through the support of various individuals and institutions. The journey of writing this book stemmed from my doctoral research at Bristol University, and continued in 2016 when I was a visiting researcher at Durham University. I thank Professor John Carpenter of Bristol University and Professor Simon Hackett, Durham University, for their continuous support and constructive feedback in this work. I also thank my employer, Universiti Utara Malaysia, and the Ministry of Education Malaysia for giving me the opportunity to take a year off work in 2016, which allowed me to ponder, start, and write the book. My deepest gratitude also goes to the University Center for the Child and Family (UCCF), University of Michigan, Ann-Arbor for the training I had, the therapists who lent their voices, and to my friends and family members, particularly my late Mum and Dad.

To Nurin and Qhadijah – my angels who inspired me to research on attachment

About the Author

Yusmarhaini Yusof is Senior Lecturer in Social Work, Universiti Utara Malaysia and mother of two daughters. Her background includes Visiting Researcher at Department of Sociology (formerly known as School of Applied Social Science), Durham University, UK, and Officer at the Women's Affairs Department, Malaysia. Yusmarhaini received her B.A in Psychology and M.S.W (interpersonal practice and mental health) from the University of Michigan, Ann Arbor. She has co-edited two books on social work published by UUM Press in 2005 and trained as a therapist at the University Centre for the Child and Family (UCCF), University of Michigan Ann Arbor.

1

Introduction

Whether you are a student, a beginning practitioner or an experienced therapist or counsellor, you have probably come across individuals, couples, or families with whom you find it challenging to develop an effective working relationship or 'therapeutic alliance'. If so, this book is for you.

This book examines the concept of therapeutic alliance and how it is understood in individual and couple or family therapy. I go on to consider the evidence from the perspective of clients, as well as from the perspective of therapists and counsellors, to support the proposition that the alliance is the key to good outcomes. This brings the person of the therapist or counsellor into play – it is my contention that in 'knowing myself', I can become a more effective practitioner.

The crucial link I am making in this book is between the therapeutic alliance and the concept of adult attachment. Attachment postulates that we bring with us our learned experiences in forming relationships and that therapists and therapy can be the 'safe haven' for clients to explore or repair problematic or ruptured relationships. To become an effective practitioner, you need to consider your contribution that may lead to a successful or failed relationship.

Through understanding our experiences in our family of origin, and, in particular, our 'attachment style' as an adult, we can learn to recognise when our own issues intrude in the therapeutic relationship. And, it is this self-awareness that is one of the key ingredients in building good rapport with clients from diverse backgrounds and concerning various issues.

Regardless of your years in practice, or if you are a beginning therapist or someone who would like to learn about attachment and the family of origin issues, this book is suitable for lay persons, educators, practitioners to supervisors, and those involved in an array of health and social care practices from various therapeutic orientations. It can be useful to a novice or an experienced practitioner in reflecting on your own practice in learning about the self or on becoming a therapist. In cases when therapists are 'stuck', attachment issues might shed light and provide a new lens to 'being stuck,' which may reflect the association between feeling or being stuck with the attachment theory. Our attachment 'insecurities' are easily activated or heightened in the event of actual or perceived threat. Therefore, knowing and learning about the self are important ingredients that benefit anyone, especially those in the helping professions.

As you read through the chapters, you will find that this book is suitable for individual or group learning. For instance, it can be used in group teaching sessions or in supervision because it covers issues concerning therapeutic development and therapists' self-development. It combines the theoretical and research literature on adult attachment and the therapeutic alliance with therapists' own voices. Throughout the book, I use the term 'therapist' to illustrate the therapists' narratives. Although the book is based on research conducted with family therapists, the experiences described are not confined to family therapists alone and apply just as much to other helping professionals working with individuals, couples, and families, such as social workers, counsellors, psychologists, or mental health professionals.

Thus, this book is written for all helping professionals, particularly therapists and counsellors, to explore the concept of attachment in building relationships with their clients. It draws on a documented journey of 13 therapists who told their stories about how they built their relationships with clients drawing from cases that they brought into a research study. Their voices illustrate how their personal and professional experiences intertwined in their development as therapists. Through the therapists' accounts, I aim to provide you with an understanding of how the self of the therapist, particularly the adult attachment style and family of origin experiences, has an impact on the relationship the therapist builds with clients. You will have the opportunity to learn from therapists with different attachment styles about their experiences of alliance building.

This book will be useful for you if you work as a therapist, social worker, counsellor, psychologist, or other member of the helping professions who offers interpersonal or therapeutic work to individuals, couples, or families. I hope that this book will appeal to helping professionals across the spectrum and that the experiences of the therapists illustrated in this book resonate with you. I hope that it will enable you to reflect on your practice and learn from it, regardless of whether you are a novice or an experienced practitioner, and whether you are still in training or aspire to become a practitioner.

While previous books have looked at either the attachment theory or the therapeutic alliance, this book offers a different perspective in that it combines the literature of both with a presentation and analysis of therapists' narratives, to provide insightful knowledge concerning the interplays of these theories. My intention in writing this book is to delve into the heart of building and sustaining therapeutic relationships through an understanding of how the self of the practitioner matters in creating change. I hope that you will enjoy the book as much as I enjoyed researching this topic.

This book starts with a chapter on alliance building and therapy. The concept of alliance from the perspective of individual and family therapy and studies related to both is discussed. The alliance in individual therapy is more straightforward than in couple and family therapy as these involve many people. In individual therapy, a therapist usually works one-on-one with the client whereas in family therapy, the whole family is involved. Hence, alliance building in family therapy is quite complex.

Subsequently the book informs the reader as to why therapists need to know about attachment and the self of the therapist. It tries to engage the reader into looking at the findings regarding the factors that are important to becoming a 'good' therapist. It elaborates on one of the factors in particular; namely, the therapist's adult attachment style. Readers are then presented with a review of the literature concerning the attachment theory and its development. The various definitions of attachment styles are provided based on previous studies, and the link between attachment and therapy is explored.

What comes next is the impact of the personal in the professional world. Readers are introduced to findings from research concerning what motivates people to become therapists before readers encounter the role that the family of origin and critical incidents in the family life of therapists have on their therapeutic work. Therapists' narratives showing the difference in the style of presentations based on their attachment styles and how personal experiences have an impact on their therapeutic work are also presented. In this chapter, the idea that the therapist is able to be an 'internal observer' to his or her past challenges is demonstrated through the therapists with illustrations of various attachment styles, which then leads to the importance of understanding the self of the therapists in practice. Therapists with 'secure' attachment styles illustrate the ability to put one's personal experiences into perspective and use them to guide their work.

The book then focuses on three aspects of alliance building in therapy: engagement, emotional connection, and safety within the therapeutic system. Examples of therapists' voices are used to illuminate the roles that therapists play in building engagement, creating an emotional connection, and providing safety within the therapeutic system. The accounts of therapists illustrate the differences of the bond factor in alliance building whereby secure therapists are able to connect better with their clients.

Finally, the book concludes with a chapter concerning the importance of continuous training and the role of supervision in therapy. The book captures in therapists' own voices the importance of supervision, showing the parallel of having a good mentor and becoming a good therapist.

The book draws on a wide range of literature from people like John Bowlby, Mary Main, Chris Fraley, Peter Fonagy, John Byng-Hall, Allan Schore, Mario Mikulincer, Phillip Shaver, Arlene Vetere, Rudi Dallos, Valentin Escudero, Myrna Friedlander, and Laurie Heatherington, as well as contributions from many other researchers in attachment and alliance. It also draws on my own research on family therapist attachment styles and their therapeutic alliances and covers a range of literature from several therapeutic disciplines including social work, counselling, sociology, and psychology. Throughout the chapters, you are invited to complete a series of exercises that can be used individually in supervision and training to reflect and learn. The exercises draw on your insights and require you to reflect on your formative experiences and their role in building relationships. Exercises are based on case studies or personal reflections that aim to promote self-development. Therapists, novice and experienced, may be susceptible to vicarious trauma or compassion fatigue when dealing with clients' issues that require empathic responses. Thus, you may find that some of the exercises provide tools to help you in your self-care. It is hoped that this will be beneficial for your continuous training as a therapist. Key summaries of important points and chapters are embedded throughout the book.

From practice to research

The participating therapists in this study were therapists identified as registered family therapists. The list of participants was generated from those who were registered through the UK Council for Psychotherapy (UKCP). From the database, invitations to participate in an online survey were issued to therapists with email addresses. Additionally, the invitation was advertised in Context, the magazine for family therapy and systemic practice. From this, 82 individuals responded to the survey. Subsequently, follow-up interviews were conducted with 13 therapists.

I am forever indebted to them as they opened their busy practices to research, especially to a study that delved into the self of the therapists, which I imagine might have been particularly challenging for some. Additionally, answering personal questions relating to their practices might also have presented difficulties for some therapists.

My encounters with the therapists made me aware of the complexity of conducting research that relates closely to one's sense of identity and professional work. Hence, I tried to put myself in the therapists' shoes. In doing so, I noticed how uncomfortable personal questions were to some therapists, as the tables were now turned, and, instead of being the interviewer, they themselves were now in the 'hot seat'. Thus, being flexible and gauging the suitability of when difficult questions should be asked helped to address the procedural and technical challenges.

Among the participants were those who seemed to struggle with questions relating to their personal experience, and thus I allowed the therapists time to answer difficult questions and respected their silence. I also realised that I brought into the field my own background and identity, which differs from the UK mainstream culture. The process of my interviews with the therapists deepens our understanding of how therapists might relate to clients, especially when their 'insecurity' is activated, suggesting that attachment styles do play a role in therapeutic alliances.

I travelled to the venue suggested by the therapists to carry out the interviews. Most interviews took place in either the therapists' homes or other locations, such as a café or a hotel lobby. I used two recording devices to capture the conversations and the interviews usually lasted for about 60–90 minutes. According to Silverman (2010), the interviewer is an active participant. Hence, I was the 'research instrument', and, in the interviews, I was very aware of the sensitivity of the subject matter and my own influence in the setting. Because I am not local, I have a different English accent and I wear a *hijab*, I anticipated that some therapists would be curious about my own background (Yusof, 2012a & 2012b). I was very mindful throughout the process to gauge participants' readiness before asking questions that might make some participants uncomfortable. Thus, the focus was on building rapport before penetrating deeper into the subject matter. I found this quite helpful in engaging participants and as a way to lessen their anxiety, as well as mine.

During the interviews, I kept a note of the nonverbal cues, such as 'moments of silence', 'facial expression' and therapists' willingness to explore the subject matter. Consideration was also given to pauses, nonverbal gestures, and emotional expressions.

Personal reflection

This book draws upon my research on therapist attachment styles and therapeutic alliances in family therapy. I cannot write about the effect of the personal to the professional self without revealing some aspects of my own personal journey. The interest in this area probably started at an early age, when, as a young child, I was the point of reference to both friends and family. This continued into adulthood when I was consulted for advice. The interest continued to grow, which then led me to choose psychology and subsequently social work as a major in college. I must point out that back then in Malaysia, my awareness of therapists and other professionals in the helping professions was mainly from movies, and I had little idea about the prospect of becoming one in my own country. Nevertheless, I was always intrigued by how the professionals whom I watched in movies assisted their clients. An opportunity arose when I received a scholarship to the United States and was given a choice to choose an area of interest, and one of the available choices was psychology. Though many around me at that time rejected the idea because of cultural norms in which people rarely sought a therapist unless medical attention was warranted, and there was a lack of job prospects in this area back home, I decided to accept the offer. I could now say that, at the age of 17, the prospect of studying abroad was far too enticing to dismiss. However, I never once regretted my decision – in choosing to read psychology, and later social work, and in studying abroad.

To fast forward, my work at the Malaysian Women's Affairs Department broadened my understanding concerning the plight of women and the issues concerning women's development in my country, and, later, my formal training continued in a child and family therapy centre in Ann Arbor, Michigan, a place where the language and culture is very different to my own. Initially, I thought my previous undergraduate training in the US and my work experience would have been sufficient to prepare me for the new adventure. But, little did I know that the 18 months' field work in an outpatient child and family mental health centre would challenge every aspect of my personal and professional development. This was the beginning of a journey that further sparked my interest in therapy and therapeutic relationships. As a young intern, I was eager to enter into therapeutic work and provide the best care for the clients who were assigned to me. Enthusiasm soon turned into doubt – doubting my own capability as a beginning therapist because most of the clients I saw started to drop out from their sessions. I started to ask questions, such as, what went wrong? What could I do to keep them engaged in therapy rather than to drop out? It was questions such as these that led me to think of the things that we can or cannot control in therapy and to realise that these include the therapist's characteristics. For example, a therapist's characteristics are uncontrollable traits; hence, what could make a difference, when 'relating' or 'engaging' with clients, that could go beyond one's external appearance. Think of your own client engagement, and whether it is easier when there is some similarity between you, as the therapist, and the client, such as cultural similarity or having a similar background.

However, there are also variations and differences within the same cultural context, and it would be naive to assume that a therapist and a client who share similarities should be well engaged. The elements of age, social class, and religion, to name a few, are some of the factors that might either unite or separate us from our clients.

Nonetheless, there are characteristics that surpass all these, such as empathy and understanding, that are essential in building relationships. Thus, as humans, we bring with us the experiences, the teaching, and the upbringing that we acquire from an early age, which theorists such as Bowlby and Ainsworth have termed 'attachment'. Attachment, which is the focus of this book, proposes that we are the product of our interactions and relationships with our parents, and, as adults, we bring with us ways of relating that are imprinted on us and that might either aid or hinder our capacity or ability to build good relationships. Of particular interest here is the therapeutic relationship, better known as the therapeutic alliance. Hence, what makes a therapist? And, what makes a good therapist?

Essentially, my employment at a university as a social work educator has influenced the way I view therapeutic relationships. In teaching the foundation course in social work practice to social work students, I think that relating to clients very much involves knowing the self of the therapists. Some years later, I had the opportunity to study for a PhD in England and to carry out research on therapy. It was in Bristol that I was able to pursue my interest to research in this area. I attended several conferences on attachment and therapy and through various readings and discussions with my supervisor, I was convinced that attachment is important in the therapeutic relationship. This further deepened my interest in the subject matter, and I started to look at how the therapists in my study used their experience – good and bad – in shaping their work. I soon learnt that 'good' attachment does not necessarily mean that everything is 'perfect' in one's life but that it is the work involved in the aftermath that defines a person's security. Attachment can be disrupted in many ways along the continuum of our life – the death of loved ones, divorce, a chronic illness, or loss can all disrupt our attachment styles. For a therapist, the professional support to continue in this demanding and challenging work is equally important and the role provided by a supervisor will provide an understanding of things that we are unaware of or miss due to our own 'blind spot' when dealing with clients and our own personal issues that might influence our work.

Hence, the passion to research this issue grew because it lent me an understanding of the things that I have been through and helped to put things into perspective. Losing a spouse through divorce and the idea of an 'ideal' family many years ago challenged how I view things, which very much revolves around attachment. In the event of a loss, our attachment insecurity could easily be activated, and, at that point in life, I could easily have lost myself in self-pity, but what kept me moving was the many attachment relationships that I have; with my God, my parents and my siblings, who continue to support me, and my supervisors and friends. Looking back, I must say that having a supportive environment is a protective factor as well as a relief. Of importance is my role as a mother to two young girls, which is a crucial aspect that motivates my interest to understand attachment and relationships. Having grown up with two supportive parents, I felt a sense of remorse at what I have to put my children through. My wish to understand the impact of the loss and to make sense of the experience led me to attachment theory. Looking from a learning perspective, it is essential to understand the formative influences of my development as an author, in which I think the readers might benefit. It seems judgemental to rate therapists as 'secure' or 'insecure' and rather 'impersonal' and 'fraudulent' to write about attachment styles and not be doing some soul searching myself. This very much relates to understanding as much as possible the key influences in a therapist's development in becoming an effective practitioner.

You could say it is therapeutic in its own sense to be able to see things from the lens of a researcher in terms of how the therapists, the experts, dealt with life challenges. Perhaps the interviews I had with the therapists provided new perspectives on my own drama, parallel to the notion that providing therapy can be therapeutic for a therapist when the therapist change happens unintentionally due to client – therapist interactions (Rosenblatt, 2009). In theory, therapists should experience therapy as therapeutic, and there are many ways to conceptualise therapeutic work. Therapy could be seen as the intersection of personal drama and self-development, and, even though the focus is on the client's drama, this might also have an impact on the therapist, and, at times, cause the therapist to reflect on what is going on in their own life. Although many therapists keep separate personal issues from client issues, they may gain perspective from helping and listening to clients talking about their struggles and finding ways to solve them (Rosenblatt, 2009). Gaining perspective from clients or learning from clients involves being sure of the co-construction that both the therapist and the client provide in their interactions, that is, the new input or meanings that these exchanges suggest. A secure therapist might welcome this interaction whereas an insecure therapist might see the challenges as a threat, which brings us to Fonagy's (2007) concept of mentalization, that is, the understanding of one's behaviours and their impact on other people and vice versa.

It is through the interviews that I had with the therapists who took part in my study that this concept of mentalization was crystallised and became much clearer to me. I came to understand the uneasiness that some therapists had concerning the 'subject matter' and my role as an outsider in interviewing the therapists about their work, and I had to challenge my own biases and limitations, especially when some of the therapists' stories mirrored my own. I also understood the 'subtle' uneasiness or curiosity that I posed by my appearance as a Muslim woman in a hijab. Through the journey of researching this issue, I started to explore one of the therapist's characteristics, the role of attachment style in fostering an alliance, especially a therapeutic alliance.

2

Alliance Building

This chapter focuses on

- a review of therapeutic alliance;
- the importance of alliance in therapy;
- the alliance in individual versus family therapy;
- the construction and outcome of alliance in individual therapy; and
- the construction and outcome of alliance in couple and family therapy.

Case Study 2.1 | Marcia Lee and the Chang Family

The therapist meets the Chang family, who are self-referred due to their eldest son's problems with the school. Daniel Chang, a 15-year-old high school student, was recently expelled from school due to some 'misunderstanding' with the school. Daniel is an A student but was expelled because he wrote an online blog venting his frustration with his friends who cheated in the school exam. Daniel, on the other hand, did not score an A for the test. In his blog, Daniel vented that he 'felt like killing those who cheated' at school. Several of Daniel's close friends reported him to their teacher about what he had written, and the school decided to expel Daniel due to safety issues.

Daniel's dad, Dr Sunil, migrated to the UK to pursue his career in medicine, and met Daniel's mum, Alicia, while attending college. They got married and have three children, 15-year-old Daniel, 13-year-old Priya, and 10-year-old Anil. Both parents are very invested in their children. The therapist assigned to this family soon realised that Daniel's problem stemmed from an intergenerational issue and an attachment issue between Daniel and his parents. Daniel's parents are both first-generation migrants who managed to assimilate in the local culture and excel in terms of achievement and pursuing their dreams. Working hard and being 'the best' are salient in their household, and the children receive the best education and attend various extracurricular activities.

An interview with Daniel revealed that Daniel felt pressure to be the best and he felt 'that he was failing his parents when he got a B in the test'. Further exploration showed that the parents' drive to be perfect stemmed from the hardship they faced when they first relocated to the UK. In addition, Alicia suffered with postpartum depression after giving birth to Daniel and could not care for him for the first two years of his life. Alicia relied on her mum, Mrs Yu Chow, who recently died due to cancer. The passing of Mrs Yu Chow was a heavy blow to the family, especially to Daniel who doted on his grandmother. Daniel reported feeling 'lost' after his grandmother's death and reported that his parents did not understand him.

The therapist, Marcia Lee, is from a biracial background and her parents were also first-generation working-class migrants from China. After listening to the Chang family, Marcia experienced a strong countertransference that made her reflect on her own childhood and how working hard and succeeding are very important to her family. To make matters worse, Marcia also lost her grandmother about two months ago. This was very devastating to Marcia who grew up mostly with her grandmother since both her parents had to work most of the time. Marcia nevertheless realised the difference between her upbringing and that of her clients and was able to empathise with Daniel and assist him in voicing his concerns to his parents. Marcia's work included repairing Daniel's relationship with his parents. Despite her strong reaction to Daniel's story, Marcia was able to remain objective and used her life experience in her professional role as a therapist. Marcia treated Daniel as the 'expert' in his problem and did not minimise the Changs' struggles. Marcia attributed her ability to face her clients to her close network and supervision. They helped her to process her countertransference when her attachment insecurity was activated upon hearing clients' issues that mirror her story line.

The intergenerational and relationship issues faced by the Chang family are not unique to this migrant or biracial family. Many families face multiple challenges. It is probably also not unique that they were paired with a biracial therapist of an Asian background, as an agency usually pairs clients and therapists based on commonalities or similarities. Even though pairing based on similarities might be helpful, such action can prove disastrous when transference or countertransference might be too high for both parties. Transference on the part of the clients, and countertransference experienced by therapists, originates from the psychodynamic perspective that looks at issues that stir or evoke strong reactions or emotions in the relationships between therapists and helping professionals, on one hand, and clients, on the other. I believe that understanding the concepts of the attachment theory leads to knowing the self that can help to regulate heightened feelings when in turmoil or stressful events. My own research and that of others indicates that helping professionals are able to deactivate their attachment insecurities and seek support when in distress if they are able to process their issues or problems. Hence, understanding one's own formative experience and providing new narratives to challenges might help therapists in their work. Exercise 2.1 aims to make you relate and think about how you might react when in Marcia Lee's situation.

Exercise 2.1 Stepping into Marcia Lee's Shoes

Based on the case study, step into Marcia Lee's shoes and imagine yourself as the therapist facing similar issues:

1. Would you seek support to process your feelings or countertransference?
2. If yes, who would you approach?
3. If no, why not?
4. When attending to a client, do you think feeling at ease is important in relationship building? Why?

How does knowing your own attachment help in creating an alliance?

Like the Chang family, there is always the notion of 'not knowing' and 'interpretation' when entering therapy. Therapists have minimal knowledge of the clients in their first encounter and vice versa. Nevertheless, the therapist might be in a better position as he or she is in a much better standing in terms of the client – therapist 'power' relationship. The 'power imbalance' needs to be addressed at the outset of therapy; if it is not, it might be a barrier to what otherwise could be a good working relationship. There are many ways in which therapeutic relationships can be disrupted or severed. For example, it could be contributed to by either the therapist or the client, as shown in the case study above. Marcia Lee can potentially sever the relationship between herself and her clients if she is unable to process her feelings and reacts negatively to her clients' stories. As therapists, we would want to minimise the error on our part and minimise our contribution to a rupture of the alliance.

Exercise 2.2 Building Your Own Therapeutic Alliance

Think of your own relationships with your clients:

- What works in building a good therapist – client relationship?
- What does not work?

For example, in building a good therapeutic relationship, some say that showing respect and dignity by acknowledging the client as the expert in his or her own issues empowers the client. The Marcia Lee case study illustrates how Marcia treats her clients with dignity by acknowledging them as the experts in their problems. This helps to foster a better therapist – client relationship, as the therapist withholds making assumptions about the client's strengths and weaknesses and their ability or disability to handle their issues.

What is the therapeutic alliance?

Having answered the questions above, let us look at the meaning of the therapeutic alliance. What is the 'therapeutic alliance'? The therapeutic alliance is the 'quality and strength of the collaborative relationship between [the] client and the therapist' (Horvath and Bedi as cited in Friedlander et al., 2006, p. 15). This collaborative bond between the therapist and their client is regarded as an essential factor in the effectiveness of psychotherapy (Krupnick et al., 1996).

The concept of alliance was established on the basis of the work of earlier theorists, starting with Freud (1912/1940 as cited in Friedlander et al., 2006) who identified transference as a central component in psychotherapy:

> 'In contrast to the patient's real feelings about the analyst, transference was the patient's displacement of feelings, impulses, and needs toward significant others on the analyst.'
>
> (Friedlander et al., 2006, p. 16).

Subsequently, Sterba in 1934 followed by Bibring in 1937 challenged the notion that everything that clients feel is transference, hence establishing the groundwork for the alliance concept to flourish (Friedlander et al., 2006). They provided an explanation of the role of positive identification with the therapist in aiding clients to accomplish therapeutic tasks, focusing not merely on transference but also on the 'reality-oriented adaptations and the real aspect of therapeutic relationship' (Friedlander et al., 2006, p. 16, Safran and Muran, 2000). However, it was Zetzel (in Safran and Muran, 2000) who formally discussed the importance of the alliance in therapeutic intervention. Zetzel believed that the alliance, stemming from the client's early developmental experiences, is the ingredient that allows clients to form a stable, trusting therapist – client relationship (Safran and Muran, 2000).

As the alliance theory has developed, many theorists have put forward various conceptions of alliance. Some of the elements discussed relate to the client's ability or capacity to bond with the therapist and/or descriptions of the client – therapist emotional bond. In addition, several new terms have been coined that relate to alliance, such as 'ego alliance', 'working alliance', and 'therapeutic alliance' (Friedlander et al., 2006, p. 16).

Various measures have been utilised to assess the alliance from different theoretical orientations, with the general conclusion that the alliance is, indeed, related to the therapeutic outcome. Martin et al. (2000), in their meta-analysis, confirmed that the direct association between the alliance and outcome supports the hypothesis that the alliance is therapeutic, even without other intervening factors. In other words, their review suggests that a proper alliance, once established, would benefit the clients who would experience the relationship as therapeutic, regardless of the type of psychological intervention.

The importance of alliance in therapy

The role of the therapeutic alliance has been discussed in relation to two main debates: firstly, the importance of understanding alliance from the perspective of either the therapist or the client (Glebova et al., 2010; Bedi et al., 2005; Martin et al., 2000), and, secondly, the timing of the alliance and how it impacts on the therapeutic progress and outcome (Friedlander et al., 2006; Horvath and Greenberg, 1989; Pinsof and Catherall, 1986).

With regard to the perspectives involved, it is important to examine alliance from both perspectives because the relationship involves clients and therapists. As shown in the case study, clients have valuable information that can help shape good outcomes. Marcia Lee is depicted as an experienced therapist who managed to assess her client's experience. This is an important aspect of building rapport because failures occur when therapists are overly focused on technique and do not assess the client's experience of what is taking place (Friedlander et al., 2006, p. 21).

Thus, therapists must repeatedly evaluate their relationships with clients, as this provides the necessary checks and balances as the therapist moves along their therapeutic work. Furthermore, it could provide a better clue of where we are heading in terms of our work with clients. This also shows clients that therapists genuinely want to make the relationship work; in other words, we care about our clients and want them to benefit from their sessions. For example, let us consider when we feel poorly and have to meet a doctor. How do we feel? It is probably easier to connect to a doctor who shows warmth, takes the initiative to know you as an individual, and takes time to explain and ask about the symptoms than to a doctor who rushes and wants to get the diagnosis done as fast as possible because of the patients waiting in line.

As time goes by, we can often become 'immune' to our work, and, hence, might come across as non-empathic. This usually happens in all kinds of helping professions – doctors and nurses as well as therapists. The problem is probably more dominant if the self of the person providing help is undergoing changes or issues. Therefore, it is best to review alliance several times during the course of our work with clients and to be aware of what we bring into our work with clients.

Exercise 2.3 Reviewing the Alliance

- Do you agree that the alliance needs to be reviewed over time?
- Provide an explanation for your answer.

It makes sense that any alliance needs to be examined over time because, depending on certain variables, including factors pertaining to the therapist or client, relationships can improve or decline and even rupture. Horvath and Greenberg (1989) suggested examining the relationship between the outcome and the alliance during the early phase of the therapeutic process, between the second and fourth sessions, while Pinsof and Catherall (1986) suggested that this should happen between the third and sixth sessions.

Regardless of the time frame, it is good practice to review the alliance and how this impacts on the outcome. It is also ethical, because clients deserve the best treatment. The notions of 'attachment' and 'knowing the self', as described in the next chapter, can prove useful for therapists to self-reflect if and when they are unable to provide optimal care. Accountability to one's own practice involves knowing when and why an alliance is ruptured. Exercise 2.4 asks you to reflect on your own practice. If you are a novice who is not yet in practice or an individual using this book for self-learning, you might use the Marcia Lee case study to answer Exercise 2.4.

Exercise 2.4 Examine Your Alliance

We have looked at how the alliance can improve, decline, or rupture over time. Reflect on what might improve, decline, or rupture an alliance:

- list the therapists' factors;
- list the clients' factors; and
- devise a plan or strategy to counter the factors you have listed above.

Research shows that a good alliance involves factors pertaining to both the therapist and the client. For example, therapist factors include the ability to engage in an empathic way, showing respect and care, and the use of the self of the therapist. Both the therapist and the client need to come to an agreement concerning the goals they want to reach through the therapy. The goals are usually achievable within the time frame of the therapy, while the task involves the commitments of the therapist to deliver the service and of the client to actively participate in therapy.

What might be some of the strategies that therapists can use to foster the alliance? In terms of the therapist factors, it is best for the therapist to have professional and personal support, as suggested by the therapists I interviewed in my study when they discussed the importance of good clinical supervision. Therapists need to provide a safe space for clients to explore issues and ensure confidentiality. However, a therapist must be clear that confidentiality is not absolute when issues involving safety are concerned. Additionally, the therapist can motivate the client's participation by being clear about the goals of the therapy and how best to achieve them and to include the client in the goal-setting process. How then do alliances differ in individual and family therapy? Let us now explore the challenges of building alliances in both settings.

Alliance in individual versus family therapy

There are challenges in alliance building, as highlighted by Bordin (1979), concerning the complexity and multidimensional nature and importance of alliance in all therapeutic models. The quality of alliance, however, varies according to the relationship between 'therapists, clients and approach-specific features' (Safran and Muran, 2000, p. 12). With regard to individual therapy, the therapeutic alliance model suggests that the alliance is often referred to as the sense of working towards a goal (Bordin, 1979). Bordin (1979) operationalised the therapeutic alliance as the tasks or collaboration between the client and the therapist that involve an agreement, the development of bonds, and agreement on goals. These were considered to influence the quality and strength of all alliances.[1]

Bordin (1979) proposed that 'the working alliance between the person who seeks change and the one who offers to be a change agent is one of the keys, if not the key, to the change process' (p. 252). This basically means that therapists and clients have their own roles in the change process.

There are four main ideas in Bordin's theory:

1. An alliance exists, or is embedded in, all types of psychotherapy, and differences only exist in the type of alliance required by each psychotherapeutic model.
2. The effectiveness of a therapy partially or entirely illustrates the strength of the working alliance.
3. The demands placed on the therapist and client differ depending on the different approaches to psychotherapy.
4. The strength of the alliance is based upon the fit between the demands of a particular therapeutic alliance and the personal characteristics of the client and therapist (Bordin, 1979).

Bordin's tripartite theory has been mainly utilised in individual therapy. The development of theory concerning the family therapy alliance has been widely attributed to the work of Pinsof (Johnson and Wright, 2002). In addition to Bordin's original conceptualisation of the alliance (bonds, goals, and tasks), Pinsof added an interpersonal dimension to address the issue of multiple people in family therapy. This interpersonal dimension is categorised into four different components: individual, subsystem, whole-system, and within-system components (Johnson and Wright, 2002). Thus, the alliance in family therapy differs from the alliance in individual psychotherapy, where the family therapist needs to establish and maintain multiple alliances. Besides that, the family therapist:

> 'must also adopt a conceptual framework that accounts for the interactions within triangles or three-person systems, recognize the influence of the system operating on him or her, and appreciate how different models of family therapy define the position of the therapist in relation to the couple or family' (Rait, 2000, p. 211).

A multidimensional (both client and therapist systems are incorporated) model, the System for Observing Family Therapy Alliances (SOFTA), was then developed by Friedlander and her colleagues in the US and Spain (Friedlander et al., 2006). The development of SOFTA reflects both between-system alliances (each client with the therapist) and within-family alliances (between each family member). The authors described three tenets underlying the development of this model:

1. It is 'transtheoretical' (SOFTA is not limited to a single theoretical approach and can be utilised across different theoretical paradigms or schools of thought), reflecting Bordin's (1979) theory, where the model could fit into any therapeutic modality, collaboration, or bond between the therapist and the client.
2. It focuses on within-family alliances. SOFTA was also developed based on the premise that clients' and therapists' behaviours are observable and interpersonal.
3. It focuses on the overlap between the therapy goals and tasks (Friedlander et al., 2006).

Exercise 2.5 Building a Good Therapeutic Alliance

- Having discussed the different alliance theories underpinning both individual and family therapies, the question to ask is what makes a good therapeutic alliance.

▶

- Describe a 'good' alliance in terms of:
  a) the bond that you make with clients,
  b) the goal, and
  c) the task.
- List three challenges that a therapist faces in building multiple alliances in family therapy.

The challenges that a therapist might face in building multiple alliances in family therapy include resistance from some of the family members or difficulties in providing fair attention to each. As shown in the Marcia Lee case study, the therapist focuses on Daniel as the identified client and places less focus on other family members. Thus, in family or group therapy, the therapist needs to be objective in looking at the concerns that each member brings into therapy because there can be a tendency to take sides or lose sight of the whole picture when faced with multiple issues from each family member.

Construction and outcomes of an alliance in individual therapy

Research shows that a therapeutic alliance has a positive impact on the therapeutic outcome. The therapeutic alliance is positively associated with treatment completion (Bordin, 1979), which means the bond that a therapist has with his or her client plays a role in the treatment retention and completion. We work well with the people that we can relate to, and therapy is all about relating to another human and helping them to get back on their feet.

For example, Gaston et al. (1998) conducted a study to establish whether the alliance, or techniques used to achieve an alliance, would be predictive of the outcome in behavioural, cognitive, and brief dynamic therapy. The participants were elderly patients diagnosed with depression. They compared the alliance and technique ratings across therapy groups and found them to vary across groups. A better working alliance was observed in the more introspective types of treatment – cognitive and brief dynamic therapy. They attributed this to the nature of the two therapeutic models, which are more likely to foster the development of a working alliance as they involve behaviours such as self-disclosure and self-observation. Thus, their findings suggest that alliance building differs across different therapeutic models. However, the client – therapist agreement concerning the goals and tasks was equally predictive of the outcome across the three therapeutic models. Their results were inconsistent with other clinical trials, however, which found that alliance was predictive of outcome across all therapeutic models (Krupnick et al., 1996). This discrepancy has been attributed to the differences in the measures being used across studies.

Similarly, Krupnick et al. (1996) investigated the role of therapeutic alliance in psychotherapy and pharmacotherapy outcomes in a sample of depressive outpatients who received interpersonal psychotherapy, cognitive-behavioural therapy, imipramine with clinical management, or a placebo with clinical management. They found that the therapeutic alliance has a significant effect on the clinical outcome for psychotherapy as well as active and placebo pharmacotherapy. Additionally, their findings showed that clients' ratings concerning their contribution to the alliance were significantly related to outcome, whereas there was no significant relationship between therapists' ratings concerning their contribution to the alliance and outcome. The authors considered that the therapist factors were statistically undetected, probably because of a lack of variability in terms of the therapists' experience in their sample.[2] Hence, the effect of the therapist contributions on the therapeutic outcome might be detected if there had been more variability among the therapists, such as by including both experienced and inexperienced therapists in the study sample.

Krupnick et al. (*ibid*) postulated that the 'therapist contribution to the alliance may be salient only to a particular subset of patients' (p. 537), such as clients who lack the capacity to form therapeutic relationships or to bond. This might suggest that the contribution of the therapists to the alliance is particularly relevant when the clients are having difficulty in bonding, which further suggests the importance of the therapist's personal qualities and skills in creating a positive therapist – client relationship.

Other studies have also shown that the therapeutic alliance may be viewed differently from the perspective of the clients and the therapists. A meta-analysis of 24 studies on the relationship of the working alliance and outcomes in individual therapy, conducted by Horvath and Symonds (1991), reported a moderate but reliable association between a good working alliance and a positive therapy outcome. This showed that clients' evaluation of the working alliance has the strongest link with outcome, followed by the observers' and the therapists' reports. Clients' success in evaluating the alliance is partly due to their awareness of how they have improved in terms of collaborating and engaging with the therapists throughout their therapy sessions. Nonetheless, the meta-analysis did not consider research involving group or family treatment, as the authors stated that, during the time that the research was conducted, there were no clear conceptual differences and similarities among the working alliances in individual and family or group therapy.

Construction and outcomes of alliance in couple and family therapy

In contrast to the one-to-one client – therapist relationship of individual therapy, establishing therapeutic alliances in couple and family therapy is more challenging due to the multiple actors involved, as well as the conflicting motives that might underlie the group dynamics of couple or family therapy. According to Friedlander et al. (2006), the work on alliance in couple and family therapy has received far less attention than the research and practice of alliance in individual psychotherapy. Several explanations have been offered regarding this; for example, Johnson and Wright (2002) commented that there is a problem in applying Bordin's tripartite of bonds, tasks, and goals to family therapy due to the issue of multiple alliances.

Compared to one-to-one work between the therapist and the client in individual therapy, family therapy comprises multiple individuals, namely, the therapist and different individuals in the family. Additionally, there is the possibility of forming a therapeutic alliance with each individual in the family and the possibility of establishing alliances with subgroups within the family, such as the parents or the children and even with the entire family as a whole (Pinsof, in Johnson and Wright, 2002). Johnson and Wright (2002) suggested that Bordin's theory does not take into account this element in family therapy and, thus, the theory should be revised to make it relevant to family therapy. In addition, an alliance can be jeopardised even before the first session begins if there is an external intrusion into the family, such as from school or Child Protection Services (Friedlander et al., 2006).

However, despite these challenges to the establishment of alliances in family therapy, research has shown that the early development and maintenance of an alliance in couple therapy (Johnson and Talitman, 1997; Knobloch-Fedders et al., 2007) and group marital therapy (Bourgeois et al., 1990; Brown and O'Leary, 2000) produces a positive outcome.

Many researchers (Robbins et al., 2006; Pereira et al., 2006) have highlighted the importance and complexity of a therapeutic alliance in family therapy. Their findings have reinforced the importance of studying patterns of alliance that rely on the successful formation of multiple relationships, such as in family-based therapies. Robbins et al. (2006) suggested that the ethnicity and gender of therapists are less relevant than their behaviour. Thus, how therapy is done is more important than who carries out the intervention. Although it would be inappropriate to generalise from one study carried out with a particular population in one cultural context, I think it is worth noting that the next chapter, on attachment, redirects us again to the importance of the therapist's behaviour in creating alliances.

If a therapist's unchangeable trait characteristics, such as gender and ethnicity, are less relevant in the success of alliance building, what are the factors that might impact on alliance building? Dunkle and Friedlander (1996), in their study on the contribution of the extent of the therapist's experience and personal characteristics to the working alliance, found that the therapist's level of experience was not predictive of clients' ratings concerning the goal and task components of the alliance. However, the personal traits of therapists, such as showing more social support, less hostility, and greater comfort with closeness, were predictive of the bond component. The authors asserted that their results are consistent with Bordin (1979), who 'maintained that therapists, like clients, bring to the therapeutic relationship a personal history that affects their interactions' (Dunkle and Friedlander, 1996, p. 459).

Other research has also shown that therapists' factors, particularly the 'self of the therapists' such as their attachment, and therapists' respect for clients, play an important role in the client – therapist relationship (Bachelor, 1995; Diener and Monroe, 2011).

In addition, Karver et al. (2006) showed that some of the best predictors of youth outcomes were the therapist's direct influence skills and therapeutic alliance with the young clients. Thus, the authors suggested that certain therapist behaviours, such as warmth and empathy (interpersonal skills), might influence therapeutic outcomes.

In the hope of further deepening our understanding of the therapeutic alliance in conjoint treatment, Beck et al. (2006) interviewed clients in four families over the course of their therapy.[3] This study focused on the shared sense of purpose about the needs, goals, and value of therapy, split alliances with the therapist, and sense of safety within the therapeutic context. Within-system alliance (such as the family's shared sense of purpose about the need, value, and goals of therapy) was reported to be the most important factor for participants. Despite clients' lack of focus on the between-system alliance, they reported that strong alliances between the therapists and families occurred when there was a good emotional connection with the therapist, when clients were confident in the therapist's ability to create change, and when there was an agreement with the therapist concerning the goals. Thus, I hope by now we can confirm the importance of the therapist factors in building the alliance, which suggests a need for more research on the factors that relate to the self of the therapist.

Additionally, Escudero et al. (2008) used SOFTA (Friedlander et al., 2006), to rate positive and negative alliance behaviours from the video-recordings of 37 families. Overall, their findings showed that, in estimating the family's improvement, the alliance-related behaviours of each family member (engaging in therapy, connecting with the therapist, feeling safe in therapy) were important aspects in the beginning of therapy, but behaviours reflecting a strong shared sense of purpose were more crucial later in the therapy (Escudero et al., 2008). As the study focused on clients' alliance-related behaviours, the researchers suggested that future research should examine the therapists' contributions to the alliance.

The studies discussed, in both individual and family therapy, suggest that the therapists' observable characteristics, such as gender, ethnicity, and experience, were less important than the therapists' use of self, such as their ability to show empathy and support. Yoo et al. (2016) suggested that the client's first impression of the therapist matters and that there is a need for the therapist to pay immediate attention to alliances from the very beginning of therapy. This suggests that inexperienced therapists may struggle as compared to their experienced counterparts.

Does this mean that inexperienced therapists lack the capacity to form a good therapeutic alliance compared to their experienced counterparts? Yusof and Carpenter (2016), in their qualitative study, showed that experience might not be the only factor that eases a therapeutic relationship and that the therapist's attachment security was also a factor. A secure therapist relates better to his or her client, which may suggest that, regardless of experience, alliance can best be fostered if a therapist is able to use his or her experience in the 'correct' and reflexive way and not let it hinder the therapist – client relationship. The concept of attachment is discussed in Chapter 3, where we look at attachment and whether attachment is fixed or can be changed.

Chapter summary

- Therapists' observable characteristics, such as gender, ethnicity, and experience, were less important than the therapists' use of self, such as their ability to show empathy and support.
- Alliance building in individual therapy is different than in family therapy, as family therapy is more complex with multiple alliances.
- Like experience, attachment style is another factor that eases the therapeutic relationship. Different to experience, which postulates that the length of experience plays a role in building a good therapeutic relationship, attachment style argues that regardless of experience, therapists are able to build a good therapeutic relationship if their attachment style is secure.

Notes

1 Bordin's definition has been 'the most heuristically rich and influential model of the alliance in conjoint as well as individual psychotherapy' (Friedlander et al., 2006, p. 16).
2 Their sample comprised only experienced therapists who had received extensive training and met the competency criteria.
3 Three data sources were triangulated – post-session interviews with each family member, observations of in-session client behaviours, and client self-reports.

3

What Therapists and Counsellors Need to Know about Attachment

This chapter focuses on

- the therapists' characteristics as important factors in therapeutic relationships;
- the idea of the therapist-in-practice not as a blank canvas;
- a summary of attachment theory from Bowlby onwards; and
- attachment styles and their various definitions.

Case Study 3.1 | Getting to Know Marcia Lee, the Therapist

You probably remember Marcia Lee, the therapist who worked with the Chang family. Marcia Lee has been in practice for over 20 years. She is an experienced therapist and has worked with various clients' issues, particularly concerning migration and trauma. Marcia Lee's family migrated from China, and Marcia Lee is a successful second-generation migrant. Despite the hardship that she experienced growing up, Marcia was raised by loving and understanding parents. Marcia understood the value of hard work as she was reminded about it all the time. There were times in her teens when she felt pressured because performance was quite central to her family's narratives. Marcia said that the turning point in her life was when she was caught sneaking out at night with her friends. She thought that her parents would punish her, but instead they reasoned with her. Her mum broke down in tears and told Marcia her fears and dreams. The parents explained to Marcia their hardships and that was the first time in their lives that they opened up to Marcia. Marcia also broke down in tears but finally understood her parents. That was when she started to express her own fears of letting them down. This was a poignant encounter in Marcia's development.

The Chang case evoked strong feelings as Marcia Lee was reminded of her own experience. Due to her years in practice, Marcia Lee realised the 'threat' of counter-transference. Fearing that this might interfere with her work and judgement, Marcia Lee turned to her colleague and supervisor for support. She reflected on the importance of understanding her parents' migration and their hopes to her supervisor.

Marcia Lee's encounter with the Chang family is a reminder of the frailty of alliance building. A therapist with no insight and self-understanding might rupture the alliance. Marcia Lee's experience shows the importance of continuous professional development and self-reflection. Based on the case study above, self-reflect and think of your own work to answer Exercise 3.1.

Exercise 3.1 Self-Reflection

- Think of your work and list the effective skills or positive characteristics that you have in working with clients.
- Now, imagine that you are entering therapy: what type of therapist will make you want to stay in therapy?
- List several important characteristics that you think a therapist should possess. Why? Are there differences between the characteristics that you list for yourself and the ideal characteristics that you think a therapist should have?

Therapists' characteristics

Now that you have listed a number of characteristics that you deemed important, what do other people tell us about the importance of therapists' characteristics? My own review of the literature shows that therapists' characteristics are crucial in alliance building. Over 20 years ago, a groundbreaking study on psychological treatment of depression in the United States attempted to examine the influence of therapist experience on the outcomes of therapy (Blatt et al., 1996). The researchers found significant differences in therapeutic efficacy among therapists, even among experienced therapists. Interestingly, according to them, differences in therapeutic efficacy were not related to the therapists' level of general clinical experience in treating depressed patients, and were independent of the type of treatment provided. Furthermore, therapeutic efficacy did not differ according to age, race, sex, religion, or marital status. So, we might then ask, what is actually important?

In one particular study, Beutler et al. (1986) proposed a model that you might find helpful in understanding therapists' characteristics. According to them, therapists' characteristics can be divided into four quadrants, as shown in Figure 3.1. It is interesting that they acknowledged that many therapists' variables are highly inter-correlated and difficult to separate, so that a classification of therapists' variables needs to distinguish between variables that have an impact on the treatment process and those that are independent of or coincide with the treatment relationship. The taxonomy needs to consider that therapists' variables differ in how directly they can be observed. Extra-therapy characteristics normally exert an unplanned effect as we cannot possibly control for certain factors like age and ethnicity, whereas those that are therapy specific, such as the therapist's experience and training, are traits that are within our capacity to control and can be used to facilitate therapeutic exchanges. Therefore, looking at the taxonomy, we could assume that therapy-specific characteristics, such as those in quadrants III and IV, are controllable by the therapist, whereas extra-therapy characteristics, such as age and emotional well-being, represent less controllable traits. This is interesting, and it is essentially good for therapists to understand that we might not be able to control everything so that we do not berate ourselves when things go wrong. However, what does research tell us? What is essentially more important in building the alliance?

In relation to the model proposed by Beutler et al. (1986), Dunkle and Friedlander (1996) conducted a survey in the United States involving 73 therapists in 15 university counselling centres and six training clinics to examine the contribution of the extent of the therapists' experience

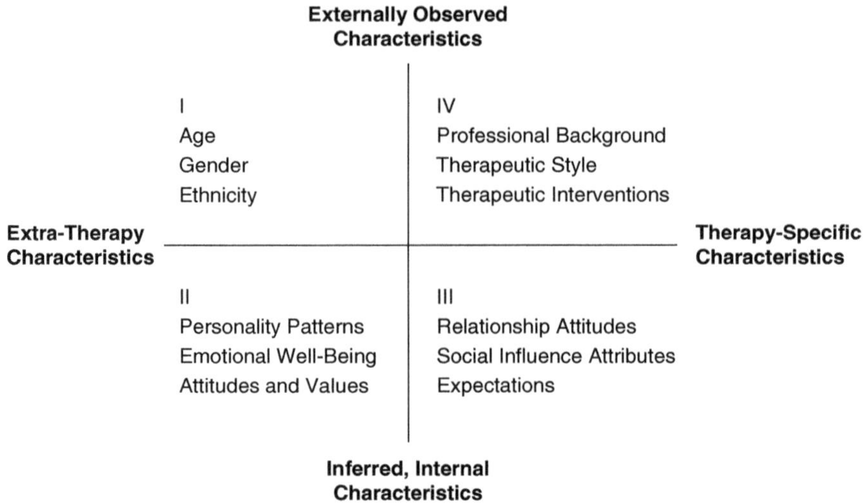

Figure 3.1 Therapist Characteristics (Beutler et al., John Wiley and Sons, 1986)

and personal characteristics to the working alliance. They found that the therapists' level of experience was not predictive of clients' ratings on the goal and task components of the alliance. However, therapists' personal behaviours and traits, such as showing more social support, less hostility, and greater comfort with closeness, were more important in building rapport. Their findings are similar to Bordin's research (1979), which showed that therapists bring to the therapeutic relationship a personal history that affects their interactions, just like the clients do. Hence, this tells us that things that we can observe externally like age, gender, ethnicity, and therapeutic interventions are less important in alliance building as compared to characteristics that are inferred and internal like our relationships, attitudes and values, and emotional well-being. Thus, we need to work on our inferred, internal characteristics that might have an impact on our relationship with clients.

Other studies, for example Ackerman and Hilsenroth (2003), noted that specific therapists' personal attributes, such as honesty, friendliness, warmth, empathy, flexibility, interest, and trustworthiness, play a role in the therapist – client relationship. Their review of the literature also shows that therapeutic techniques that increase the ability of the therapist to connect with the client, such as being active in therapy, facilitating the expression of affect, and attending to clients' experience, which foster a comfortable therapeutic environment, were important aspects of alliance building. Other researchers have also touched on the importance of therapists' variables or roles on the outcome of psychotherapy. For example, Najavits and Strupp (1994) found that therapists labelled as 'effective' by clients, other therapists, independent observers, and supervisors displayed more positive behaviours, such as warmth, affirmation, understanding, helping, and protecting, than negative behaviours, such as belittling, blaming, attacking, and rejecting. It is also interesting that therapists with a higher score for helping alliance showed more warmth and friendliness, as well as being more affirming and understanding, when compared to their counterparts who were rated low on helping alliance. Thus, this means that therapists should take into account the influence of personal characteristics on their role as providers of support.

Reflecting on my own experience, when I first started my training in a mental health outpatient centre in the United States, I was in difficulty because most of the clients dropped out of the sessions after their first meetings. My reaction as a novice back then was to attribute this to my external appearance: I was young, inexperienced, Asian, in a foreign environment with a different accent and different externally observed characteristics – such as gender, age, or ethnicity – as stated in the Beutler et al. model (1986). Additionally, I was not doing well as a beginner for a number of possible reasons, such as my lack of experience while at the same time trying to pave a way in learning how to become a therapist and learning how to build a good therapeutic alliance in a new cultural context. From the literature, we could conclude that my personal experience that clients choose or would relate better to therapists who are similar to them did not hold true. It might be an added bonus to share similarities, but, most importantly, are the inferred internal characteristics, such as warmth and understanding.

Now, looking back, I was probably trying too hard to connect with my clients while also trying to do the administrative part, such as explaining about informed consent and the rules and procedures that might have come across as 'insecurity', as it looked pretty formal, staged and rigid before I gained confidence in working with clients. This gradually became easier with plenty of training and clinical supervision. Is my journey reflected in others' work? Blatt et al. (1996) also noted that even when only providing clinical management to individuals receiving a placebo, a clinician could be effective, suggesting that 'the therapeutic alliance established by a talented clinician may be an essential component of effective treatment' (p. 1282). This again indicates that the personal qualities of the therapist are among the most important influences on therapeutic outcomes.

Therapist-in-practice

I have now suggested that therapists' characteristics like warmth and understanding are more important than their age, gender, or ethnicity. The ability to convey warmth and understanding partly depends on self-awareness, an important concept in a therapist's development. A novice therapist often does not realise the impact of his or her personal experience or use of self when working with clients. This therapist often operates based on experience and common sense, rather than using clinical theory or skills when in practice (Donati and Watts, 2005).

As this novice therapist progresses and later develops to become an experienced therapist, the therapist soon realises the impact of the personal on the professional self. Further self-development work allows the experienced therapist to develop a harmony between the personal and the professional self (Donati and Watts, 2005). Thus, this enables the experienced therapist to navigate through therapy, and understand when to use his or her personal self, such as personal disclosure, appropriately. The distinct difference between a novice and an experienced therapist lies in the ability to use the personal self, clinical theories, and skills constructively, with minimal interference of countertransference. The experienced therapist understands what might trigger insecurity, as illustrated by the therapists whom I interviewed in Chapters 4 and 5. These therapists also know how to manage and when to seek support. Now that you know about therapists' characteristics and self-awareness, Exercise 3.2 invites you to explore your own self-awareness or insights regarding your personal development.

Exercise 3.2 Are You Self-Aware?

Either as a novice or experienced therapist or as someone interested in exploring the impact of the self, think about whether you understand the impact of the factors listed below in shaping your development:

- your personal history;
- your family;
- your strengths;
- your weaknesses; and
- your environment (this may include your place of work, your neighbourhood, your place of birth, your country and nationality, or other factors that you think are relevant to your development).

Nevertheless, it is undeniable that therapists, like clients, do want to feel comfortable in therapy. How do we achieve this? The therapeutic relationship is a two-way process. Acknowledging that help is needed is probably less threatening than feeling that you are in a mess and that you can no longer control the situation (Sands, 2000). Hence, for many clients, therapy is probably an ending as well as a beginning: an ending to coping on their own, and a beginning in letting a third party – the therapist – into their life. This requires trust by both parties and it is the ability to provide safety to clients that might be a challenge to any therapist as both clients and therapists have preconceived ideas and expectations concerning how a 'client' or a 'therapist' should be.

In her book *Falling for Therapy*, Sands (2000), a sociologist, stated that most therapists in practice are well aware that they can never be a blank screen. She explains in her own words that therapy or the 'field of enquiry' will inevitably be 'contaminated' (p. 19). Therapists' outlook on life, their temperament, personality and presence, and their behaviour towards each client will have an impact on their clients directly or indirectly. Hence, in practice, therapists can never be a blank screen, as we have our own experiences and bias that we bring into our work. She further argues that this will be shaped by our training, which very much influences the way we as therapists see and hear our clients.

Thus, it would then be an advantage for a therapist to know what might help or hinder the therapeutic process by consciously knowing what he or she brings into therapy. This will ensure that the therapist is taking care not only of the client but also of himself or herself. Additionally, it is probably difficult to build a therapeutic relationship if the concern is more on diagnosis and the therapist fails to provide a safe space for clients to feel accepted and connected. This very much boils down to the therapist factors, such as skill, personality, and temperament. Therapeutic relationships can be non-therapeutic and feel 'fraudulent' to clients in a subtle and obscured way rather than in a revealed, complex way due to the power imbalance between the therapist and the client. However, a sense of inequality in therapeutic work can be avoided if we do not confuse inequality and difference (Sands, 2000). This depends on the way therapists relate to clients and vice-versa. Normally, we could assume that clients will be 'uncomfortable' when they first enter therapy as they are opening their souls to an outsider or an 'expert', and it is the therapist's way of relating to clients that will make therapy less threatening. Relating to anyone depends on how safe we feel with the environment as well as the perception that we build based on the aura that exudes from the person. In making the personal relationship with the client workable, sometimes the therapist needs to pursue issues about which the therapist himself or herself feels incompetent, powerless or exposed (Vandenberghe and Martins da Silveira, 2013). To do this, therapists need to be comfortable, and knowing ourselves is an essential ingredient to feeling safe.

McGoldrick (in Pieterse et al., 2013) stated that self-awareness involves the relationship between our beliefs, values, worldviews, and life experiences, and how they affect our knowledge and understanding of ourselves. Self-development is often the result of therapists undergoing training, not integrated or embedded in therapists throughout training (Pieterse et al., 2013). Hence, for continuous development, therapist training should integrate exercise components that focus on the self of the therapist. Lennie (2007) described the complexity of a self-development group as a method to know oneself. This probably relates to the challenges posed in a group dynamic. Working on the self is an intense introspective exercise – the therapist needs to challenge his or her bias, and understand the effect of his or her upbringing and surroundings. I believe that this can be achieved through personal therapy, as discussed in Chapter 6. In this book, I aim to show how self-awareness or knowing ourselves is very much related to our 'adult attachment styles'. Let me begin with some background on attachment theory.

Attachment theory and later development

Attachment theory as it applies to infants and children may be well known by many readers, but because it is central to the ideas contained in this book, I think it bears restating here. The theory was originally developed in the 1970s by the psychiatrist and psychotherapist John Bowlby (Bowlby, 1973, 1980), who proposed that our cognitive, emotional, and social development occur within the context of relationships with significant others (Dolan et al., 1993, p. 409). The theory provides a foundation for understanding the development of emotional attachment in children; conceptualised as an affectionate bond that the child forms with a caregiver who he or she turns to in times of distress (Bowlby, 1973). As a result of interactions with caregivers, children develop internal working models about others and themselves (Dolan et al., 1993). The internal working models contain beliefs about the attachment figure and the child, which guide the behaviours and expectations in the parent – child relationship. A child's working model of self is a belief that he or she is worthy of care and deserving of others' help, while the child's working model of others stems from the belief that caregivers will be responsive and nurturing (Bretherton, 1985). For example, a child learns to respond based on the feedback received from the attachment figure. Therefore, attachment will be maximised if the child is able to predict the response of the attachment figure (Shilkret, 2005). If an attachment figure like a mother or a father is unpredictable in the way she or he responds to the child, the child might be ambivalent in seeking the attachment figure's support in times of crisis, hence creating insecurity. Thus, attachment is seen as a secure base for the child to explore the world, as well as a safe haven from which to seek comfort when the child is in distress.

Attachment, or the bond that we have with attachment figures, is gradually embedded during childhood, and internalised and organised into personality patterns that guide later adult relationships. An individual who grows up in a supportive, loving and caring home is more likely to grow up with confidence, knowing where and when to seek support or protection, whereas an individual who is less fortunate is more likely to view the world as 'comfortless and unpredictable, and they respond either by shrinking from it or doing battle with it' (Bowlby, 1973, p. 208).

Another monumental study was an observational study by Ainsworth and her colleagues (1978), who further expanded the attachment field. They described the 'secure style' in which a child showed signs of distress when separated from a caregiver and left with a stranger. Upon seeing her mother, the child would hold her for a period of time, and then be able to resume her play, exploring the environment in the presence of the mother. Another two types of attachment described by Ainsworth et al. (1978) are the 'avoidant' and the 'anxious/ambivalent'. Children with avoidant attachment styles would remain physically distant in the presence of their mothers, rarely cry upon separation, and, once reunited, avoid their mothers altogether or mingle close enough but greet them casually. This is in contrast to ambivalently (anxious) attached children who show some anxiety prior to being separated and become intensely distressed when separated. Upon reunion, they display a mixture of contact-seeking behaviours and resisting of contact. Subsequently, Main et al. (1985) proposed another category known as 'disorganised' attachment style where children showed contradictory behaviours, like wanting to approach the caregiver, and, at the same time, showing ambivalent behaviours.

Bowlby initially proposed that attachment patterns and internal working models of relationships were considered to be relatively stable throughout the life span; from childhood, moving to adolescence and adulthood (Bowlby, 1973). We know that attachment figures provide stability, in which they serve as a target for proximity-seeking during distress, a safe haven in time of need and a secure base from which a child or an adolescent can securely explore the outside world and know that they are always welcomed by their parents when distressed, and comforted and reassured if frightened. The availability of parents to their young children provides security for these children to grow into secure adults who know where and when to seek help when they encounter difficulties.

Schore and Schore (2008) proposed the concept of the regulation theory as an extension to Bowlby's attachment theory. They argued that affective attachment communications, which can be seen between attachment figures and a child, facilitate the maturation of brain systems, particularly the right brain, which enables attachment behaviours. Conditions affecting the initial stages of brain development, that is, the postnatal maturation of the limbic-autonomic circuits, depend largely on the caregiver's 'provision and regulation of social-emotional experiences' even though the right brain reorganises later in life and retains plasticity (Schore, 2005; Kolb and Gibb, 2011). Thus, individual development of the brain, mind, and body is interconnected and flourishes due to the relationship between the caregiver and an infant. This involves the culture and environment that either support or threaten such development. According to them, 'attachment experiences shape the early organization of the right brain' (p. 10), which is important in building the emotional sense of self, and other nonconscious activities such as intuition (Allman et al., 2005), insight (Fink et al., 2010; Grabner et al., 2007), and creativity (Bowden and Jung-Beeman, 2003; Jung-Beeman et al., 2004).

Various researchers also provided evidence that attachment occurs beyond the first year of a child's life (Matas et al., 1978; Main et al., 1985; Main and Weston, 1981; Waters et al., 2000; Zayas et al., 2011). After this period, attachment patterns are governed by internal working models that are formed based on the child's experience with the attachment figure. The internal working models can remain stable (secure or insecure attachment relations) and serve to regulate, interpret, and predict attachment-related behaviour, thoughts, and feelings of the self and the attachment figure. Thus, an individual whose parents are available and supportive as a young child will feel valued and develop a competent working model to grow into a secure adult.

Nevertheless, beyond infancy, an event sometimes affects the security of the child (Bretherton and Munholland, 1999). For example, previously supportive parents may become distressed due to sudden unemployment and might not be as empathetic and available to the child, which disrupts the child's confidence in the parents, and, hence, working models are revised. However, as a secure child, this child has the capacity to understand the temporary nature of the circumstances. Improved life circumstances or the availability of support from others will lead the child to reconstruct the working model of the valued self and caring others. This, however, is challenging for children with insecure attachment styles.

Does this mean that your attachment style cannot be changed as an adult? A longitudinal study of attachment security in infancy and early adulthood by Waters et al. (2000) showed that, rather than being stable throughout an individual's lifespan, attachment could also change depending on one's experiences. Waters et al. (2000) interviewed 60 young adults who had participated in the Ainsworth Strange Situation study (Ainsworth et al., 1978) when they were infants, and found that nearly three-quarters of the respondents received a similar attachment classification to the one given to them as infants. However, attachment stability could be disrupted by a major negative life change, such as the 'loss of a parent, parental divorce, life threatening illness of parent or child, parental psychiatric disorder, and physical and sexual abuse by a family member' (p. 685). This is an interesting study as it challenges the original notion of attachment stability proposed by Bowlby and provides evidence that even though a secure base is a stable concept in childhood and adulthood, the attachment representations can be changed in light of our real experience. This is a hopeful message for therapists and counsellors who, because of their early experiences, may have insecure attachment styles. If attachment styles are not fixed, they are 'repairable'. We will look at this issue later in the chapter.

However, in general, the attachment style established in childhood influences an individual's attachment in later life. This affects close relationships that revolve around comfort, love and security and permeates all types of close relationships, such as friendships, romantic partnerships (Ainsworth, 1989), and, as discussed here, therapeutic relationships.

Main's work on 'metacognitive functioning' – the capacity to represent past experience in a coherent and collaborative way, where life events and early relationship are given new perspective as the individuals try to make sense of their past experience to the listener – changed the course of attachment research. Coherence and the capacity to collaborate with the listeners, such as being able to provide a clear, believable and consistent narrative with insight and humour even when describing traumatic past experience, reflect the attachment security (Slade, 1999). The work of Fonagy et al. (1991) on 'reflexive functioning' is also an important development of the attachment theory. Reflexive functioning refers to 'the operationalisation of the psychological processes underlying the capacity to mentalize [which] involves both a self-reflective and an interpersonal component that provides the individual with [a] capacity to distinguish inner from outer reality' (Fonagy et al., 2007, p. 24). This acts as a protective factor against adverse childhood experience. Thus, the ability to reflect upon an experience, especially a negative experience, helps to process childhood trauma, which is crucial in the development of the secure self. Fonagy and Target (1997) suggested the ability to mentalize – to differentiate between our own perspective and others, as well as understand that people have different views, or to 'read' people – helps us in our day-to-day social context. They hypothesise that having a secure attachment enables us to read others and ourselves.

The evidence of different types of attachment styles

Attachment styles in general are 'patterns of expectations, needs, emotions and social behaviour that result from a particular history of attachment experiences, usually beginning in relationships with parents' (Fraley et al., 2000 in Mikulincer and Shaver, 2007). However, from the 1970s onwards, several definitions of attachment styles have been coined by various researchers.

George et al. (in Mikulincer and Shaver, 2007) introduced the three categorical models of attachment styles based on the Adult Attachment Interview (AAI) coding system. The Adult Attachment Interview was designed to explore adults' mental representations of attachment. Respondents are asked to recall their childhood relationships with their parents (Main et al., 1985). The work of Main et al. (1985) suggested that the attachment relationship shifts from external and observable interactions in early childhood to internally represented beliefs and expectations in adulthood. Their work was the first attempt to assess the security of the adult's working model of attachment (George et al., in Main et al., 1985). There are two premises underlying the AAI where 'autobiographical memory is the ongoing reconstruction of one's own past, in light of new experiences, and [an] idealization of the past particularly negative childhood experiences, can be traced by studying the form and content of the autobiographical narrative separately' (Van IJzendoorn, 1995, p. 388). The AAI is a semi-structured interview describing general descriptions of relationships, memories that are either supportive or contradictive, and how the interviewees describe the present relationship that they have with their parents (Van IJzendoorn, 1995). The analysis of the AAI has revealed three attachment styles: secure, dismissing, or preoccupied. Later, Main and Solomon (in Mikulincer and Shaver, 2007) added a disorganised/disoriented style. Hence, the attachment styles could broadly be categorised into two: secure and insecure.

An adult with a secure attachment style is one who is able to describe and discuss his or her positive and negative relationships in a fluent and coherent manner. Those with dismissing styles tend to normalise and provide positive descriptions of parents. Research shows that adults with dismissive styles also have difficulty in recalling childhood attachment experiences. On the other hand, adults with preoccupied styles are described as those who often show a passive, angry, and confused preoccupation with attachment figures. The use of psychological jargon, nonsense words, and occasional childlike speech are typically noted in the interview (Main, 1996). The final category is the disorganised/disoriented type, who seem to 'suffer from a breakdown of organised attachment strategies (primary, hyperactivating or deactivating)' (Main and Solomon in Mikulincer and Shaver, 2007, p 26). Their disorganised behaviours relate to the way their attachment figures respond to them, where the attachment figures seem to be disorganised and unpredictable because of their own unresolved losses or attachment-related trauma (Mikulincer and Shaver, 2007).

Hazan and Shaver (1987) subsequently introduced a three-category self-report measure of adult-attachment style in 'romantic' relationships; that is, with a close partner. This measure assesses only the way an individual views his or her experiences and reactions in close relationships, and not the individual's conscious or unconscious mind that accounts for these feelings and behaviours (Mikulincer and Shaver, 2007). It is intended to capture the three attachment styles identified by Ainsworth et al. (1978), as applied to adults, which are as follows:

- Secure – 'I find it relatively easy to get close to others and am comfortable depending on them and having them depend on me. I don't worry about being abandoned or about someone getting too close to me.'
- Avoidant – 'I am somewhat uncomfortable being close to others; I find it difficult to trust them completely, difficult to allow myself to

depend on them. I am nervous when anyone gets too close and others often want me to be more intimate than I feel comfortable being.'

- Anxious – 'I find that others are reluctant to get as close as I would like. I often worry that my partner doesn't really love me or won't want to stay with me. I want to get very close to my partner and this sometimes scares people away.'

Brennan et al. (1998) later developed the Experiences in Close Relationships (ECR) measure by factor-analysing items from all the self-report attachment measures that had been created in the late 1990s and found two factors – anxiety and avoidance – that were common to most measures and that could also place a person in the two-dimensional space (model of self and others). The anxiety and avoidant dimensions could be categorised into four attachment categories:

- Secure – those with positive models of self and others (low in both the anxiety and avoidant scores);
- Preoccupied – those with positive models of others and negative model of self (high anxiety, low avoidant);
- Dismissing – those with negative models of others but a positive model of self (high avoidant, low anxiety); and
- Fearful – those with negative models of both self and others (high in both the anxiety and avoidant scores).

Exercise 3.3 Reflection on Therapeutic Practice

Having read about all the attachment styles above, think of how you form your relationship with your clients. Try to answer the questions below:

- Has there been a time when forming a therapeutic alliance was challenging?
- Why do you think this happened?
- How then do we form a good alliance with our clients?

Exercise 3.4 Knowing Your Attachment Style

Having reflected on attachment styles and completed Exercise 3.3 on your own therapeutic practice, I offer two possible ways for readers to find out about attachment style – by completing the Relationship Questionnaire (RQ) below or completing a different questionnaire on a website (link provided later).

A. The Relationship Questionnaire

The questionnaire is adapted from the Relationship Questionnaire (RQ) by Bartholomew and Horowitz (1991) and will tell you about your attachment style.

Please go through each step in the questionnaire according to the sequence.

STEP 1:

The following are descriptions of four general relationship styles that people often report. Please read each description and place a tick next to the letter corresponding to the style that best describes you or is closest to the way you are.

____ A. It is easy for me to become emotionally close to others. I am comfortable depending on them and having them depend on me. I don't worry about being alone or having others not accept me.

____ B. I am uncomfortable getting close to others. I want emotionally close relationships, but I find it difficult to trust others completely, or to depend on them. I worry that I will be hurt if I allow myself to become too close to others.

____ C. I want to be completely emotionally intimate with others, but I often find that others are reluctant to get as close as I would like. I am uncomfortable being without close relationships, but I sometimes worry that others don't value me as much as I value them.

____ D. I am comfortable without close emotional relationships. It is very important to me to feel independent and self-sufficient, and I prefer not to depend on others or have others depend on me.

STEP 2:

Now please rate each of the relationship styles above to indicate how well or poorly each description corresponds to your general relationship style.

▶

Attachment Styles	Disagree Strongly			Neutral/ Mixed			Agree Strongly
Style A	1	2	3	4	5	6	7
Style B	1	2	3	4	5	6	7
Style C	1	2	3	4	5	6	7
Style D	1	2	3	4	5	6	7

STEP 3:

Calculate your underlying attachment dimensions using the following equations:

- Self-Model = (style D) + (style C) MINUS (style A) + (style B).
- Other Model = (style D) + (style B) MINUS (style A) + (style C).

STEP 4:

Plot your scores along the two scales – self-model and other model – to yield your attachment style in the chart below.

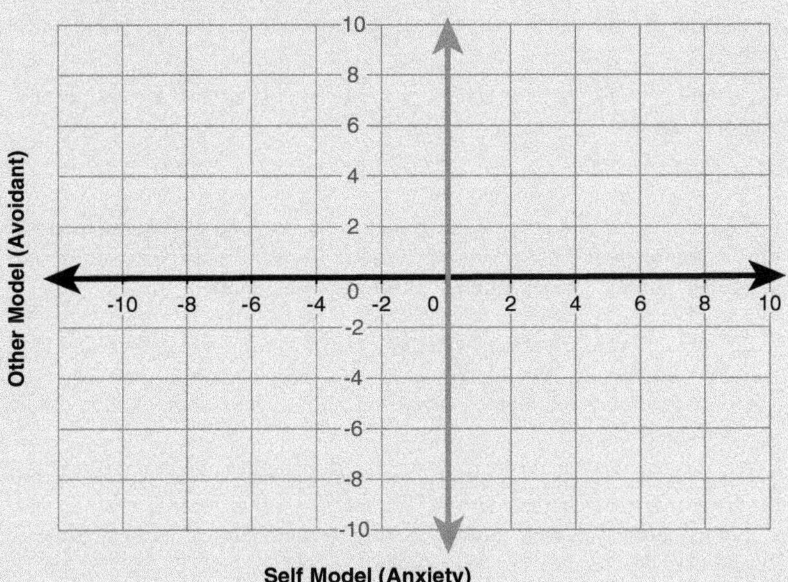

◀

Explanation of your attachment style

Do not read this section until you have completed the exercises above.

Step 1:

You have just completed the RQ developed by Bartholomew and Horowitz (1991). The RQ is a self-report attachment style questionnaire in which you are given a choice to select one of four attachment styles that best describes yourself:

Style A: Secure

Style B: Dismissing

Style C: Preoccupied

Style D: Fearful

Step 2:

These ratings provide a profile of an individual's attachment behaviour.

Step 3:

Self-Model: A higher score refers to higher anxiety and a more negative model of self.

Other Model: A higher score refers to higher avoidance and a more negative model of others.

Step 4:

A negative model of self is closely linked to anxiety, and a negative model of others is associated with avoidant behaviour. The anxiety and avoidant dimensions could be categorised into four attachment categories:

- Secure – If your attachment anxiety and avoidant scores are low (i.e., minus scores on both dimensions), this suggests that, generally, you are comfortable expressing emotions and do not worry about others rejecting you.
- Preoccupied – If your score for attachment anxiety is high (i.e., a positive score) and low in attachment avoidant (i.e., a minus score), this suggests that, generally, you tend to worry about the availability or responsiveness of your partners' support and fear rejection.

▶

◀

- Dismissing – If you score higher (i.e., a positive score) in the avoidant dimension, and low (i.e., a minus score) in the anxiety dimension, you generally prefer not to rely on others.
- Fearful – If you score higher (i.e., a positive score) in both the anxiety and the avoidant dimensions, this suggests that you are uncomfortable depending on others or providing attachment for others.

Further explanation:

This questionnaire is designed to measure how you relate to other people, otherwise known as the attachment style. People differ in the way they relate to other people and how they think of close relationships based on two underlying dimensions: attachment-related anxiety and attachment-related avoidance. People who are more anxious than others worry about others' opinions of them and are afraid of rejection, whereas people who score lower on this dimension worry less about such matters. In contrast, people who score higher in attachment-related avoidance are less comfortable with depending on others. Hence, they keep to themselves and are less able to open up to others.

This is important because it will hopefully help you in managing conflict and your relationships with clients in your therapeutic work. By knowing your attachment style, you will be able to realise when your attachment insecurity is activated in challenging situations, and, hence, be more prepared when facing such challenges.

B. Online Attachment Questionnaire

In addition to the RQ, if you are interested in further exploring your attachment style, I would strongly recommend that you visit Dr Chris Fraley's website, www.labs.psychology.illinois.edu/~rcfraley/index.html#about. Dr Fraley is a professor of psychology at the University of Illinois in the USA and is one of the world's leading experts on adult attachment. Dr Fraley offers free access to two validated online questionnaires that measure attachment styles and close relationships. Visit www.web-research-design.net/cgi-bin/crq/crq.pl. This will provide you with two options using the Experiences in Close Relationships-Revised (ECR-R) questionnaire (Fraley et al., 2000). I recommend Option A, which is more comprehensive and which you can complete, and, if you choose to, will allow you to track your attachment style and personality functioning across time. The survey is easy to complete and automatically generates charts to show your attachment style and provides further explanation on your attachment style and personality.

Activating our attachment system

Human beings are biologically equipped to survive in our environment. Our bodies and behaviour are automatically activated in the presence of real or perceived threats. For example, we will strive to find a safe place that we call 'home', and, once this need is met, we will automatically feel safe and at ease. The purpose of the behavioural system is to ensure our survival, continuity, and reproduction, and one of the fundamental behaviour systems is the fear system (Howe, 2011). Think of what fear does to us. Too much fear will heighten our insecurities, which might then lead to anxiety, whereas having a little bit of fear or stress is good as this is what motivates us and keeps us moving and achieving. Similarly, when people are presented with threats, their attachment systems are activated. What do we do then when this happens? Bowlby's attachment theory (1973, 1980) outlined that the attachment system will be automatically activated upon the appearance of a physical or psychological threat. Imagine a young child being frightened: the child will automatically seek comfort and solace from his or her attachment figure.

As an adult, the mental representation of the attachment figure acts as a schema in maintaining proximity, safety, and emotional support, and the adult will now have more attachment figures, such as friends or intimate partners. The new attachment figure, such as a relationship partner, should accomplish three functions in order to be an attachment figure. The first is proximity maintenance, in which people turn to and seek closeness to their partner in times of distress and need. Next, the partner functions as a safe haven, who alleviates stress and provides support. Finally, the partner acts as a secure base who allows the engagement of nonattachment behaviour, such as exploration in order to develop a unique, autonomous personality (Mikulincer et al., 2002). Thus, in the event of threats, our attachment systems are activated. What will we do in the event of real or perceived threats? We usually seek support from people we are close to, i.e., we turn to our attachment figures. The triggers that lead to threats can either be attachment related, such as a new love that is a threat to the current partner, or attachment unrelated, such as a car accident. When attachment systems are activated, the availability and responsiveness of attachment figures provide security, comfort, and relief. This is automatically conducted by our brain by accessing our attachment-related mental contents, such as thoughts of our attachment figures, which leads to action, such as seeking contact (Mikulincer and Shaver, 2007). Therefore, attachment insecurity is heightened in events in which no attachment figure is available. However, in adulthood, our ability to gain security could be from mental representations of the attachment figures, such as positive memories that we have, without even having to seek physical proximity. Nevertheless, gaining comfort from a mental representation of our attachment figures might not be enough to provide adequate comfort in extreme conditions such as serious illnesses or traumas, and, in these situations, attachment activation can trigger proximity-seeking behaviour irrespective of our age (Mikulincer and Shaver, 2007).

What is the relationship between our attachment styles and attachment-system activation? For individuals with secure attachment styles, the threats encountered evoke positive mental representations of the attachment figures, such as support, love, and positive interactions with the attachment figures. However, for individuals with insecure attachment styles, the threatening situations will increase access to negative thoughts or memories, and attachment behaviour will be either deactivated (avoidant) or over-activated (anxious). For example, anxious attachment styles will cause attachment behaviours to be over-activated, which intensifies the individual's vigilant monitoring of the attachment figure's behaviours and the increased likelihood of detecting real or imagined signs of distance, rejection, or unavailability because the attachment figure is not consistent and not always immediately available. In one study, children with secure attachment styles remembered positive events more accurately than negative events. They also had greater competence to understand negative emotions and their consequences, which the author suggests warrants further exploration of the representational features of attachment and social representation (Thomas, 1999). This provides some evidence that those with secure attachment styles have the confidence to seek support when needed and regulate emotions better in social representation, including in times of distress. Attachment styles also determine the use of security-based self-representation (an aspect of oneself resulting from positive upbringing or interactions) when facing stress (Mikulincer and Shaver, 2007). For example, an individual with a secure attachment style is able to recall his or her positive interactions and memories, and feel valued and loved, which provides comfort under stress. From the positive interactions, an individual with a secure attachment style develops a positive sense of self, such as feeling capable when facing threats. Furthermore, the availability of attachment figures in modelling positive caregiving, such as showing empathy and kindness, act as protective factors that can be modelled internally, where a secure individual is able to treat himself or herself in ways similar to that of the attachment figures – with kindness, empathy, and understanding – when they gain autonomy as an adult. Hence, in the event of threats, the secure individual will be able to regulate his or her emotions, maintain emotional stability, and activate self-caregiving routines similar to those of his or her attachment figures in coping with difficult situations.

Attachment theory and therapy

What can research tell us about attachment theory and therapy? Some authors proposed how attachment theory is positioned between the therapist – client relationship. For example, Sauer et al. (2003) examined the relationship between client and therapist attachment orientations, and early working alliance, and their findings showed that, over time, therapists' anxiety negatively affects the working client – therapist alliance. This supports Bowlby's attachment theory as a framework to explore the 'relation between client and the therapist interpersonal stances and the development of the working alliance' (Sauer et al., 2003, p. 372). Sable (2004), in her article on attachment, ethology, and adult psychotherapy, additionally suggested that psychotherapy offers the experience of an attachment relationship where working models are re-assessed and revised to provide a new narrative to old perspectives or stories. An individual's attachment behaviours provide clues as to how the person relates to other people. This includes how emotions are regulated and memories are retrieved. For example, Main (in Sable, 2004) explored the meaning adults give to their childhood experiences and found that security very much relates to the coherence of the narratives provided by the interviewees, and not their actual experiences. In contrast, insecure attachment is often characterised by incoherent narratives, which are manifested through inconsistencies, and breaks and disruptions in the story, and irrelevancies (Slade, 1999). For Main, the issues do not concern the type of story the individual tells but where, when, and how the story unfolds. More salient is how the story is told, and what the individual allows himself or herself to know, feel, and reflect in relaying the story. Main's work on narrative provides words to clients' emotions and experiences that elevate distress, by helping the client to gain understanding concerning their ways of relating (Sable, 2004). Hence, therapists could provide a new meaning to clients' attachment, and, by experiencing a new secure attachment and composing a consistent narrative, the client is able to change his or her working models by creating a positive relationship (Slade, 1999). This shows that the working model could be changed.

The study of Schore and Schore (2008) demonstrates that the right-brain-to-right-brain communication system between a caregiver and an infant involves various right-brain nonverbal cues, such as recognising emotion and auditory perception. For example, a secure attachment style is likely to develop when a child perceives positive attachment behaviours, such as pleasant intonation pitch and friendly facial expression. The ability to self-regulate emotion depends on attachment communication (Schore and Schore, 2008; Schore, 2005). Thus, a child with an insecure attachment style may face various relational challenges in adulthood. However, this is repairable through the therapist – client relationship. Schore and Schore (2008) proposed an attachment-based clinical approach that focuses on the unconscious nonverbal affective of the right brain rather than the conscious verbal left brain in working with clients. They aptly stated that 'all techniques sit atop these right brain implicit skills, which deepen and expand with clinical experience: the ability to receive and express nonverbal affective communications; clinical sensitivity; use of subjectivity/intersubjectivity; empathy; and affect regulation' (p. 16).

Thus, in terms of the attachment perspective, therapists act as a secure base and through the therapist – client interaction and relationship, the therapist models to the client new ways of relating. Nevertheless, to model this new way of relating or providing a corrective experience, the therapists themselves need to feel secure in therapy in order to attend to clients' narratives on what can and cannot be told and to emphatically challenge clients' old ways of destructive thinking and provide new narratives. Modelling a new way of relating very much relates to Bowlby's (1988b) view that the therapist's emotional availability is important in helping clients to heal in therapy as clients who seek therapy might have faced various issues such as rejection and abandonment. Thus, successful therapy occurs when a therapist is able to provide a secure base for clients to explore their problems and to achieve solutions (Dunkle and Friedlander, 1996). This is similar to Dallos and Vetere's (2009) Attachment Narrative Model (ANT) that focuses on important stories that we develop about our connections (emotional, sexually intimate relationships, attachment with others, dependencies, experiences, and expectations of trust in our relationships), where our childhood experiences form the material of our developing narratives about ourselves and others. These narratives are then transferred to other situations and relationships outside our family.

The ANT model also depicts that narratives are dynamic, similar to the therapeutic process; they change through constant construction, reconstruction and review and evoke strong feelings. Thus, we choose where to tell our stories, who to tell, what to include or exclude, and what we want others to know. Hence a secure base is important for us to be able to open up in discussing our issues; to challenge our current views by exploring within a systemic framework looking at every system involved, such as our patterns of relating and attachment, and to reflect upon them. Perhaps the ability to consider an alternative story, reflect on feelings and provide a corrective measure concerning the way we deal with our challenges shows how secure therapists challenge their own problem-saturated stories and reconstruct new narratives that enable them to look at their problem with a bird's eye view, from a third person's perspective (Yusof and Carpenter, 2016).

One might question whether it is necessary for therapists to be secure themselves to do this. Caring for another is not an easy task; some people struggle to do this task for various reasons, including the inability to connect or be emotionally present. Therefore, the therapist has a paramount task to connect and relate, and, together with the client, find ways to solve the client's issue. The therapist – client relationship requires an emotional connection, and the ability of the therapist to be empathic, convey sensitivity, and provide a safe space for clients to explore their issues relates to the therapist's attachment style. Imagine having a volatile client in therapy; what might be your reaction? How do you think the therapist's attachment style might play a role? The therapist's role towards the client can parallel aspects of the caregiver's care for her child. Thus, a secure trait is more desirable as therapists will probably be more available emotionally to their clients, able to provide a safe space, and will not easily be ruffled by the clients' drama. In contrast, insecure therapists, despite good intentions, might not be able to provide the best care due to their own unresolved issues. According to Farber and Metzger (2009), counsellors or therapists need to embody the characteristics of secure attachment figures in order to provide a safe space for client exploration although they themselves might not possess all the characteristics of secure attachment from early life experience. Therefore, one suggestion is for therapists or any professionals in helping professions to work continuously in building and developing the secure selves of the therapists.

Exercise 3.5 Strategies for Creating a Secure Base for Clients

Based on the research that has been reviewed, how are you able to provide a secure base for your clients? List at least three strategies that have worked for you.

Looking at Bowlby's therapeutic tasks in Table 3.1, other than a secure base, the therapist is more likely to be able to assist clients towards a better change if he or she is able to encourage the client to reflect on how their reaction and action might be due to past experiences and recognise what is helpful or unhelpful in contributing to the client's present situation. Hence, by doing this, the therapist is also challenged by his or her own capacity to be available to clients and to model the positive experience of the relationship that the client might take as a new narrative when the therapy has ended.

In line with this, in the last 20 years the way in which we view therapeutic work has changed. Most therapists acknowledge clients as experts of their own problems, which balances the power dynamic in the therapeutic relationship. Hence, therapy is viewed as a two-way relationship in which both the therapist and the client co-construct meaning and affect each other in their exchanges. Nevertheless, we cannot overlook the idea that some clients seeking therapy are looking for an attachment figure. Farber et al. (1995), for example, advocated the idea of the therapist as an individual who is perceived as 'wiser and stronger' (p. 206). According to them, this notion is further strengthened through the role, status, and education that the therapist possesses.

Table 3.1 Bowlby (Routledge, 1988a) Five Therapeutic Tasks (p. 138)

First task	To act as a secure base or a sounding board that allows the client to explore difficult issues that would be impossible for clients to discuss without encouragement or support from someone who the client could trust (the therapist).
Second task	To assist the client in their exploration of past and present relationships, their expectations of their own feelings and behaviour and those of others, and their unconscious biases.
Third task	To encourage the client to examine the relationship between the therapist and the client. This acts as a model of a constructive relationship.
Fourth task	To encourage the client to reflect on how their reaction and action (perceptions, expectations, feelings) might be due to past encounters, especially with their parents.
Fifth task	To enable the client to recognise images or models of themselves and of others, derived either from past painful experiences or from parents' misleading messages, which might or might not contribute to their present situation.

However, some clients might not regard their therapists as wiser and stronger due to their own past experiences, while others might be ambivalent or have feelings of gratitude towards their therapists. In both cases, therapists are functioning as the new attachment figure, similar to parental attachment, which evokes anxiety and ambivalent feelings (Farber et al., 1995). Nonetheless, clients may devalue their therapist or therapy or might resist therapeutic intervention to defend themselves against the anxious and ambivalent feelings stirred up by this new attachment figure. Hence, in this particularly challenging situation, it is the role of the therapist as an attachment figure to provide support and acceptance despite being regarded as a threatening figure by the client, which could shift the therapeutic relationship from negative to positive. The shift to find a solution for this disparity is an integral aspect of therapeutic change, where the supportive and nurturing environment provided by the client – therapist relationship is often a good avenue for working collaboratively towards achieving a common goal.

Within the field of family therapy, Byng-Hall (1995) discussed the role that the therapist plays in stressful situations in which a family therapist can become a temporary attachment figure to clients similar to Bowlby's therapeutic task. The aim is to use therapy as a secure base to 'assist the family to explore ways of improving [the] security of the family's attachment network' (p. 51). The idea of the therapist and therapy as a secure base has given rise to narrative perspectives in attachment work (Vetere and Dallos, 2008). The therapist in this context provides a secure base for clients to tell their stories. For example, therapists with secure attachment styles, as shown by previous research (Dozier et al., 1994; Black et al., 2005; Yusof and Carpenter, 2016), were able to build better therapeutic alliances with clients compared to their insecure counterparts.

Perhaps this is where the notion of the therapist as an attachment figure providing safety to the client is important, because therapy reconstructs past negative experience and provides a space for reflective functioning that gives new meaning to the client's current issues. Our past attachment experiences, particularly our interactions with our parents, shaped our ability to reflect on experience and provide coherent narratives about our lives (Main et al., 1985; Crittenden, as cited in Vetere and Dallos, 2008, p. 375). Hence, attachment is also seen from the perspective of how people tell their stories and the content and coherence of the structure of the story (Vetere and Dallos, 2008).

Exercise 3.6 Role of the Therapist in an Attachment Perspective

What did you get from learning about how past attachment experiences shaped our current lives? Try to summarise the role of the therapist according to the attachment perspective.

Key Points 3.1

- Therapists can provide a corrective experience for clients to reconstruct past challenges.
- Despite therapy being 'temporary', and the short duration of the client – therapist meetings in therapy, therapists can become a 'new and lasting' attachment figure through which they model what and how behaviours could be corrected outside of therapy, and provide a new story, possibly a 'new and meaningful' angle different from the one that the client originally brought into therapy.

What if our attachment is insecure?

The review of the literature shows that therapists with secure attachment styles are able to provide a safe space for clients to discuss their issues (Yusof and Carpenter, 2016; Black et al., 2005; Dozier et al., 1994). In other words, they are likely to be able to be more equipped to connect with clients.

What about others with insecure attachment styles who aspire to become good therapists? It is unfair to say that therapists with insecure attachment styles do not make good therapists. Therapists, like everybody else, are human beings with past experience – bumps, twists and turns along the way. Attachment, despite its stability, might be disrupted in major life events. Additionally, we are bound by our biases, which might be displayed strongly or subtly when meeting clients different from ourselves. We might also be challenged because of the differences. It is important not to pathologise people because of their past experiences and the legacy that those experiences create in terms of attachment. At the same time, people with problems in relation to attachment could potentially experience barriers in doing effective therapeutic work. Thus, therapists with insecure attachment styles might act in a way that could disrupt the therapeutic alliance when attachment-related behaviour is activated under threat. Hence, therapists should continuously work to understand themselves better.

Nevertheless, how do we know that attachment insecurity can be changed? The social and emotional circuitry of the brain is shaped by environmental behaviour surrounding it from prenatal development and continues throughout life. Brain plasticity is a combination of the interactions between our genetic blueprint and experiential factors (Kolb and Gibb, 2011; Rossi, 2004). It refers to the growth and transformation in the physical structure, connections, and functions of the brain cells from prenatal and throughout the entire lifecycle, and during the everyday life interactions and changes in the neural networks, which relate to the psychological experiences of novelty, creativity, significant memory, learning, and behaviour (Rossi, 2004).

Neurobiological research shows the connection between social and emotional behaviour and how our brain circuits are shaped by our experiences; early experience plays an important role in our vulnerability and resilience in handling future adversity (Davidson and McEwan, 2012). Davidson and McEwan highlighted both the undesirable impact of early life stress on later development and also the protective effect of a nurturing environment. Psychosocial experiences influence the neurobiological process and can change the structure of the adult brain (Garland and Howard, 2009). The experiences gained or insights developed in various life stages have the capability of changing the working model. This relates to the idea of brain neuroplasticity, that human brains can reverse early adverse experiences with the right support (Davidson and McEwan, 2012). This could be done through training, counselling, or psychotherapy.

Moreover, we now know from our previous discussion on attachment and therapy that attachment insecurity can be gradually repaired through relational-oriented therapeutic contexts (Schore and Schore, 2008), in which the therapist resonates with the client's implicit presentations. Therapists with an understanding of the right-brain effect on attachment development would foster a conducive therapeutic attachment experience that allows clients to give new meaning to their pain. One of the proposed ways is through a therapeutic encounter that focuses on nonverbal cues, in which the empathic therapist is 'consciously, explicitly attending' to the client's verbal and nonverbal behaviours, such as changes in facial expression or posture, as well as attending to the therapist's own reaction towards the therapeutic process (Schore and Schore, 2008). Therefore, a therapist's training may include personal therapy, as discussed in Chapter 6, which can comprise attachment work.

The idea of neuroplasticity – the interaction between the brain, our thought processes, and the environment – and the fact that the brain has the capacity to heal from past negative experiences provide developmental and neurobiological evidence supporting the concept of recreating a new narrative. This is in line with Main's work (Sable, 2004) and the mentalization concept proposed by Fonagy et al. (2007), involving self-reflection and the ability to be aware of the mental states of the self and others. 'Thought, emotion, and action trigger neural activity, which can lead to a reorganisation of the brain, shaping future psychosocial experience' (Garland and Howard, 2009, p. 197). Experience includes internal and external events, such as injury effects, hormonal actions, developmental effects, aging, and thought processes (Kolb, 1995). Thus, given the right support and environment, we have the ability to teach the brain and create new stories that change how our experiences shaped our attachment styles. Having said this, therapists should be aware of their inner voices and know what might trigger their insecurities and seek ways to address this through training and therapy. Hence, being reflexive, as proposed by Fonagy et al. (2007), is part of the training that should be embedded in therapists' daily practices.

Chapter summary

- Therapy can act as a secure base for the therapist – client relationship.
- Attachment, despite its stability across the lifespan, could be disrupted in later life due to major life events. The secure base built during childhood will be a buffer for any calamities one might face in later life. However, the narratives we build when we are young are dynamic due to our brain plasticity and can be changed through constant construction, reconstruction, and review. Thus, finding a secure base, irrespective of whether it is from parents, intimate partners, close relationships, or a therapeutic relationship, will enable individuals to open up in exploring their issues and in reconstructing a new narrative.
- Being reflexive is associated closely with a secure attachment style.
- Being reflexive acts as a protective factor against adverse childhood experience. This helps to process negative experience, which is crucial in the development of the secure self.

4

The Impact of the Personal on the Professional World

This chapter focuses on

- an introduction to the research findings concerning what motivates people to become therapists;
- the role that the family of origin and critical incidents in a therapist's family life have on their therapeutic work; and
- therapists' presentations based on their attachment styles concerning how their personal experiences affect their therapeutic work.

Exercise 4.1 Factors Influencing Your Therapeutic Career

Reflect on when you first decided to become a therapist or a counsellor. What led you to choose this career?

Murphy and Halgin (1995) undertook a survey of factors that influence psychotherapists' career choice and found seven factors. Rate the seven factors from 1 (Not at all like me) to 5 (Very much like me).

▶

◀

	Factors	1	2	3	4	5
1.	Professional altruism					
2.	Vocational achievement and opportunity					
3.	Personal growth and inquisitiveness					
4.	Personal problem resolution					
5.	Experiences of personal problems					
6.	Troubled family experiences					
7.	Experiences of strong interpersonal alliances					

- Based on your answers, which factors best represent you?
- There might be more reasons than the one listed by Murphy and Halgin (1995). Think of your own experience. List some reasons that led you to choose to become a therapist.

Introduction

Now that you have done the exercise above, do you think that there is any part of your personal life or the self that has had an impact on your choice of career? The Murphy and Halgin survey (1995) compared the motivations and experiences of 56 clinical psychologists practising psychotherapy and 53 social psychologists in choosing their career. Social psychologists acted as a comparison group because of their similarities to clinical psychologists with regard to educational achievement, prestige, and professional socialisation. Surveys were sent to clinicians selected from the 1992 National Register of American Health Service Providers in Psychology, while the social psychologists were selected from the membership list of American Psychological Association Division 8, The Society of Personality and Social Psychology. Interestingly, they found that clinical psychologists practising psychotherapy were more influenced than social psychologists in choosing their career due to 1) experience of psychological distress in themselves and in their families of origin, 2) a desire to resolve personal problems, and 3) a wish to pursue opportunities for vocational achievement and professional advancement compared to their counterparts in social psychology. Nevertheless, the authors stated that most of their participants did not view problematic histories as a major issue that led them to their career path. The impact that the personal has in our professional world is narrated in this chapter through therapists' own accounts. A review of several research studies concerning therapists' factors in their career choices leads to the following critical question: What impact does the personal have on our professional world?

Other than the study above, Farber et al. (2005), in their review of the empirical and clinical literature about what motivated and influenced psychotherapists to choose their career, found 12 recurrent themes:

1. Therapists' experiences of being marginalised in society lead them to think about others and their own positions or places in society. These facilitate the development of observational skills, including the wish to make the world a better place for others and a desire to help people in distress.
2. They endured painful childhood experiences. Thus, they were more aware of not only their own distress but also that of others, which greatly influenced their career choice. It is most likely that this awareness is what creates a sensitive and reflexive therapist.
3. They develop a high degree of psychological mindedness. That is, they begin early in life to think about the dynamics of human behaviours, such as why people think and act as they do, which brings them to the career path of becoming a therapist.
4. They serve as confidants to family and friends, which develops their sense of identity with the role of therapist.
5. They have good role models, for example, teachers or experienced therapists who awakened their interest in becoming a therapist.
6. Their ability to engage in personal therapy themselves and their desire to help others usually stem from early childhood motivation, such as coming from a family that likes to help.
7. The need to help others is one of the career motivations that makes them choose to become therapists.
8. They need to understand others, probably due to childhood experiences of personal or familial distress.

9. They feel a need for autonomy; many therapists think that the career is less limiting than many other professions.
10. They feel a need for (safe) intimacy, that is, they find pleasure in the therapeutic relationship.
11. They need intellectual stimulation. Many therapists pursued the career because of the intellectual challenges provided in their work as therapists.
12. They desire self-growth and healing. In hearing other's issues, questions, and ways to cope with their experiences, indirectly, therapists are also working on these issues that benefit themselves (pp. 1024–1027).

Exercise 4.2 Spot the Similarities

Reflect on the answers that you listed in the exercise at the beginning of this chapter. Can you spot any similarities between your answers and those listed here?

Interestingly, some of the factors listed in Murphy and Halgin's survey (1995) and Farber et al. (2005) are illustrated in my interviews with family therapists, where they describe their experiences of family conflict, of physical illness or death, and of mental illness in their families.

Therapists' attachment styles and family of origin

Despite the similarities with the findings from previous studies (Murphy and Halgin, 1995; Farber et al., 2005) that families of origin influenced therapists' career choices, the interviews that I conducted with 13 family therapists in the UK on therapists' attachment styles and therapeutic alliance differ in terms of the findings concerning the role that attachment styles have in therapists' lives. The interviews were part of a bigger study in which family therapists who completed an online survey on attachment styles (Yusof and Carpenter, 2012) were invited to participate in the in-depth interviews. This chapter shows narratives from selected therapists' accounts that best illustrate the issue. The participating therapists discussed their family of origin and critical incidents in their family life as a way to understand the stresses that impacted on themselves or their client families.

The interplay between attachment styles, family of origin, and our chosen profession were illustrated in the stories narrated by participating therapists. They reported that it was their need to understand themselves and their family of origin that influenced them in becoming therapists. The family of origin or the issues the therapists faced when they were growing up provided valuable insights.

Exercise 4.3 Attachment Styles and Family Experiences

How might you expect different attachment styles to relate to family experiences? Think of your own family experiences, the one you had when you were young or the one that you have now. How might these experiences impact on your attachment style and your work as a therapist?

Now that you have considered how attachment styles relate to family experiences, how is this reflected in the interviews that I carried out with therapists in the UK? One participant considered that his training as a family therapist had increased his understanding about the type of family that he came from. His reflection on his family of origin also heightened his awareness of the different types of family and its functions. In his response when asked about this, he said:

> 'Well, I guess, at the time I certainly wasn't aware of it but, certainly, after starting my training, I realised what a dysfunctional family I had (laughs). And I don't know if it's fairly common. I don't know many people who've got wonderful fully functioning families.'
>
> (Andy)

Another example is when Di described her own understanding of family upbringing in relation to how her own family experience contributed to her self-development. She reflected, after a long pause, how those life experiences provided an insight for her now:

> 'I'm sure ... (6 secs), I'm sure ... (7 secs) it does give me understanding you know of (4 secs) some particular things. Mm so it gives me an understanding of the role that children take when they have very strict or controlling parents, it gives me understanding.'
>
> (Di)

Later in the interview, she said that her work had made her think of her own upbringing. Even though she did not disclose her thoughts openly, she highlighted her thinking about her family through a series of unanswered questions to herself, which provides a sense of how one's past life experience might have an impact on the self:

> 'mmm ... (5 seconds pause) you know, also, those, sort of, you know, (voice a bit stressed) ... those, you know, I think of what kind of family we are, were we an over involved family? Were we a distant family? Were there kind of clear boundaries and limits? How did we mm (3 secs), you know, how was it, when we came to sort of adolescence and sort of the positions we were in? You know, yeah, that obviously you can see that ... I have two of my siblings are gay or lesbian and so, you know, I have an understanding mmm ... (long silence).'
>
> (Di)

Can you notice the difference between these two therapists with 'secure' (Andy) and 'insecure' (Di) attachment styles?

In general, therapists with insecure attachment styles struggled to address this issue, as noted by their silence and long pauses in the interviews, as well as their own questions about the type of families they have.

Another example, when asked whether her family of origin had an influence on her decision to become a family therapist, Izzy spoke of the importance of 'communication', and, from her illustration, it seems that a lack of communication in her family was one of the aspects that motivated her to become a therapist. In her own words, Izzy stated how:

> 'In a sense, my family didn't communicate. They didn't talk to each other. My parents were together for 17 years. They had a very intellectual and mm ... (8 secs), yeah, an intellectual relationship, but emotionally they were two worlds apart.'
>
> (Izzy)

On another occasion, Izzy reflected on her own childhood, and, in retrospect, she could see the connection between wanting to understand her family and her interest in becoming a family therapist. Once again, she mentioned her background as part of what influenced her in her work:

> '... yeah and the influence ... (6 secs) of my background was about, what could have made things better but didn't and therefore looking for that in my work with families.'
>
> (Izzy)

Izzy, in her reflection, revealed her thinking that the inability to deal with her past, 'made things better but didn't', was a factor that made her want to make families better. It was interesting how she kept going back to her family of origin and how her personal experiences played a role in her desire to 'help' other families.

The examples reflect that therapists' past experiences provided opportunities for them to develop insights to understand themselves. However, therapists with insecure attachment styles (Di and Izzy) were struggling to address this question, as noted by their silence and long pauses, as well as their own questions about the type of families they have. The secure therapists were more open in discussing the issues and using those experiences to realistically understand their present predicament.

Key Point 4.1

Therapists with secure attachment styles were able to be 'internal observers' to their past challenges.

What is an 'internal observer'? It has been described as the concept that captures the way the '... adult could observe how family life was when they were children and distinguish this from the understanding they gained through later relationships across development' (Steele and Steele, 2005, p. 157). This concept was later modified by Fonagy et al. (2007) to reflective functioning, a capacity to monitor thought processes in others as well as the self, an important concept to achieve if there was significant adversity in the past. Probably, the ability to negotiate challenges directed at the self when they were children by 'reflecting upon the actions of the adults and sibling relationships they observed' helped these children to survive and grow into a secure individual (Steele et al., 1996, p. 158).

It is important to note the difference between reflective functioning and introspection. The first is an automatic procedure that we unconsciously invoke when interpreting behaviours; our capacity to make sense of that helps to regulate behaviours. Introspection, on the other hand, is a conscious procedure that has a clear impact on the experience of oneself (Fonagy et al., 2007). Since reflective functioning is proposed to be an automatic procedure, therapists in practice then need to learn to be conscious through training and supervision of the things that might affect their practices without their realisation. This automatic procedure could be seen in some of the therapists' interviews; despite also going through a challenging childhood, they appeared to be more secure than others who had experienced difficulties. This reflects their secure attachment styles and their ability to be more reflexive in looking at past adversity and recreate new meaning or a new story that contributes to their chosen career and the way they connect with clients.

For example, Andy, whose attachment style is secure, was more open in discussing his family of origin. His laughter gave a lighter atmosphere to the whole subject and it took away some of the 'sensitivity' of the subject matter, which illustrates Main's idea concerning metacognitive functioning where this therapist was able to provide a clear, coherent, and believable narrative. Andy went on to discuss the impact of his childhood experience and how that shaped his understanding of his present family's situation. Andy, throughout this discussion, was able to show awareness of how distressing it was to grow up in a 'dysfunctional' family, but he also managed to reflect and be realistic, showing the capacity of reflexive functioning normally displayed by individuals with secure attachment styles. He illustrated how those experiences might play a role in his own worldview of his relationships:

> 'I think that's connected, in the beginning, with my need to sort out my family's dysfunctional whatever ... I think from my background thinking, I've been married for 20-something years, I've got two children and we haven't divorced yet [he was reflecting on his past struggles and how that shaped his relationship] and my sister, also. She got married when she was 18, she's now 50 something and they're still together, something about being able not to necessarily follow the patterns of previous generations. If you look back

> through my family, there's all sorts of dysfunctional or separations, divorces, unmarried mothers and so on but there's me and my sister, this generation, and they've actually done it quite differently for some peculiar reasons, I'm not sure why. Maybe through experience thinking I don't want actually to be like that, don't want our children growing up in an environment where there's arguing and so on. It's not to say that we don't argue but it doesn't resolve in major upheaval or people moving out or whatever.'
>
> (Andy)

In my study, therapists with 'dismissing' attachment styles did not touch on whether their family of origin influenced their choice of work while those in the 'fearful' attachment styles did not elaborate on this issue. This was evident in their lack of reference to their family of origin. Why was this? Attachment theory suggests that those in the fearful attachment styles are characterised as both highly anxious and highly avoidant in relationships, while the dismissing attachment styles are characterised as avoidant and less anxious. They both share similar traits in which both have high avoidance, so perhaps it is not surprising that they avoided talking about difficulties in their families or that their attachment insecurities were activated when they were questioned by a stranger (the interviewer).

Exercise 4.4 Family of Origin and Attachment Styles

Reflect on whether you have listed family of origin as one of the factors that led you to become a therapist and your attachment style. What will you do when faced with challenging situations? How would the challenges impact on the way you might respond given the situation? What would be the particular triggers that activate your attachment behaviours?

Generally, being 'invulnerable' is not a good solution. Although this might be seen as being detached from the clients, nevertheless, people showing dismissing attachment styles usually maintain composure by displaying invulnerability (Dozier and Tyrrell, 1998; Mohr et al., 2005). However, the ability to be reflexive shows that everyone can develop a secure attachment style. How do you think you might achieve this? Previous research shows that the decision to pursue a demanding profession as a therapist may be influenced by experiences of strong, interpersonal alliances, such as the experience of being a confidant to others, the experience of having a teacher or role model in one's chosen profession, and the experience of having a positive familial relationship (Farber et al., 2005; Murphy and Halgin, 1995). Hence, despite insecure attachment styles and family of origin experiences, assuming this is the reason for the insecurity, you can still draw strength from other positive interpersonal alliances, such as partners and friends, or from supervision.

Critical incidents and family life

Research has shown that critical incidents and family life are one of the motivating factors in choosing a career in psychotherapy. The Murphy and Halgin (1995) study, for example, also found that clinical psychologists chose a psychotherapeutic career because of their experiences of psychological distress in themselves and in their families of origin. This is important to note as time and time again similar findings have been found by research showing the link between the therapists' personal and professional life. Similarly, the therapists in my study showed that besides their need to understand themselves and their family, they discussed critical incidents that occurred in their family life.

Before we look at what the therapists had to say about critical incidents in their lives, try to answer the questions in Exercise 4.5.

Thinking of critical examples that lead us or shape the work that we do might be challenging to some people. Some reflection is necessary

Exercise 4.5 Critical Incidents and Career Path

Think of any critical incidents that might have led you to your chosen career. Take a minute to reflect on one of those incidents and write down the answers to these questions.

- Did the incident inform your decision to become a therapist?
- If yes, how so?
- If not, think of examples from your experiences that influence you and your work.

when you need to ask yourself about the motivation of being a therapist or staying in the career.

For example, Betty associated her motivation to do therapeutic work with the death of her mother:

> '... when I was just 18, my mother died, really quite suddenly of liver cancer, she was only ill, as far as I was concerned, for 6 months. But she died at home and that was quite a profound effect, watching my father nurse her, my sister and myself ... And so I think that's the most formative, I'm sure there's lots of other things but, you know, if I had to think back, that's what I would say, I would say that was a real change from being somebody who's going into teaching, probably PE, to move to a therapeutic stance and I think it isn't by chance that my sister is a trained individual psychotherapist working with adults. So, I think it really had a profound effect, yeah.'
>
> (Betty)

Now, let us take a look at whether this theme also resonates within the presentation of therapists with insecure attachment styles. Like Betty, Joan suspected that her father's death might have contributed to her becoming a family therapist:

> 'I suppose, the most important thing in my development, probably, was that my father died when I was 17 and I don't know whether that really influenced me to become interested in child mental health or if it was an unconscious thing. You know it was a very important part of my life and so I'm not sure. But I would, an educated guess, now, from my experience would be there was something in that, that influenced me to go into the work that I do.'
>
> (Joan)

Although Betty was categorised as secure and Joan was categorised as fearful, what was the difference between these two therapists? Did attachment styles play a role?

Exercise 4.6 List the Difference: Secure Versus Insecure

Read the excerpts from the two therapists' interviews and what you think the difference might be. List the differences. Is there more than the one you mention?

The excerpts showed that critical incidents in the therapists' lives played a role in shaping their therapeutic work. In the illustration, Betty described the scenario that she recalled when her mother was diagnosed with cancer and she watched her father take the responsibility of caring for her mother and how those experiences had impacted on her choice of career. In contrast, Joan was unsure of what had influenced her decision to become a therapist, despite realising the contribution of her father's death in her choice of work. This might relate to her insecure attachment style in that fearful attachment style is characterised as both highly avoidant and dismissing. Remember that our attachment insecurity will be activated when we are facing threats, and, in such a situation, the question posed invoked memories that might be difficult for Joan to describe; as illustrated by her response.

Like Betty, Andy highlighted an event that had a critical impact on his self-development. He speculated on whether the divorce of his parents had played a role in motivating him to become a family therapist; in his own words:

> 'I was thinking far more about my family of origin and wondering whether there's something in my need to understand my family and how things were that led me into wanting to work with families and whether it was to fix them or just to understand them, to fix them so they don't go through what I went through or to understand more about how families work and, my family, how they worked.'
>
> (Andy)

Key Points 4.2

- Therapists who were identified as secure seemed able to recall painful experiences, discuss them openly, and relate them to their present work.
- Insecure therapists also described similar experiences and highlighted family type and critical incidents in family life. The difference between the secure and insecure therapists' presentations in this study lies in the depth of their reflections. Though therapists with insecure attachment styles reported similar experiences, they did not elaborate on them and did not reflect on how those experiences affected their professional growth.

The question then is how important is the need to understand ourselves? Does this have any bearing on our work as therapists? The therapists' excerpts provide a view of the importance of understanding ourselves. Furthermore, we could see the difference between therapists with secure and insecure attachment styles in the depth of their ability to reflect and to relate the impact of their experiences on their work as therapists. Thus, based on the interviews with therapists, I recommend that therapists explore their past experience and what they bring into therapy as this might either help or hinder therapeutic alliances.

Furthermore, our stories often play a role in making us notice some things or ignore and miss other things in our therapeutic conversations with clients (Hedges, 2010). A client's story can resonate with our own, which evokes responses from our body, thoughts, feelings, and emotions (Hedges, 2010). Resonance, when used appropriately and sensitively, as shown by secure therapists, can deepen our understanding of ourselves and our work with clients. Exploring our attachment styles and knowing the interplay between our own attachment style, family of origin, and incidents in life can help to prepare therapists in alliance building in therapy.

Personal experience and therapeutic work

There is a reciprocal relationship between our professional and personal growth where we might find it difficult to separate them. The question that we need to ponder is whether we are allowing our personal experience to interfere with our work with clients. This is most likely challenging to many therapists, especially when facing a difficult situation.

Paris et al. (2006) studied marriage and family therapist interns' (trainees) experiences of personal growth. They engaged 13 interns from 10 programmes in the USA in an internet discussion forum. They explored sources of growth (i.e., what led to growth as a therapist?) and kinds of growth (i.e., how did they grow?).

They found that participants grew as therapists in terms of:

1. perspective taking, such as being able to see another person's point of view;
2. self-awareness, such as being conscious of one's own motivations, beliefs, thoughts, and actions;

3. confidence – being self-assured of one's skills and abilities;
4. letting go, involving recognising one's own limits to control other people and events;
5. clinical skill-building, such as learning to empathise, trust, and be honest;
6. knowledge building; and
7. hopefulness, which is the feeling of anticipation and optimism.

Their sources of growth included personal therapy, related work experiences, personal relationships, spiritual beliefs, and generic learning. For example, they found that difficult 'personal relationships', such as dealing with divorce and being a survivor of a family with alcohol abuse, provided insights for their participants in dealing with their own therapeutic work. The interviews discussed in this book also reveal that experienced family therapists had similar personal experiences, such as having an adopted child or a 'complaining' mother, which provided valuable insights, not only in dealing with their clients, but also in their own ability to manage their feelings and practice.

For example, therapists commented on their own personal relationships and how that related to their present job. They highlighted the overlap between their own personal life, past and present, and their role as a family therapist.

This could be seen when Andy talked about the satisfaction that he gained when families improved. He also pointed out his need to understand his own family struggle:

> '...having seen some families come from quite a difficult place to functioning much better is part of that job satisfaction and I think that's connected in the beginning with my need to sort out my family's dysfunctional whatever.'
>
> (Andy)

He went on to describe his own personal experience of having an adopted child and the struggle that they, as a family, have had:

> 'I think it, certainly, there's a bit that makes me think, mm, because in my situation we got one child who's adopted who does give us quite a few problems because he has very ambivalent feelings towards us at times.'
>
> (Andy)

He further claimed that, despite knowing in theory what needed to be done, the reality was far different. He explained how his personal struggles gave him a 'better insight' into understanding families. This excerpt illustrated the spill-over between a therapist's personal experience and his own work as a therapist:

> 'You know, although theoretically you might know how to behave or what to do, on how to help this child but when you are emotionally involved with this child it becomes much more difficult to put that into practice which gives me a better insight in working with families. This is not just about putting down on paper and say follow this program and everything will be fine, it is more difficult when you got an emotional component in it.'
>
> (Andy)

Another example of how personal experience has an impact on our therapeutic work is shown in the illustration provided by Carl. He described how having a complaining mother affected his work with someone who had a similar manner:

> 'Yeah ... and I had a really whiny mother myself ... so I think I'm a bit vulnerable to whiny mothers. I think if I'm a bit tired, then I'm not really or something else is troubling me, I found myself feeling very, very angry, annoyed with this person and being quite sharp ... anyway.'
>
> (Carl)

Subsequently, when asked what he thought about his reaction when facing such situations (complaining mothers), due to his (unconstructive) response to the situation, he reported that it was reasonable for clients to seek help from other therapists.

Carl illustrated the importance of 'letting go' or realising when to put a stop if his past experience handicapped his relationship with his clients, which, in turn, might hinder his clients' progress:

> 'Well, I don't really feel that good really 'cos I knew I was contributing to it myself ... I thought it was only fair for them to go to someone else, have another chance with someone else.'
>
> (Carl)

Key Point 4.3

Secure therapists illustrated the ability to put their personal experiences into perspective and used them to guide their work. In other words, the secure therapists, due to their family upbringing and their ability to be reflexive, were able to use their past experience and put themselves in a theoretical perspective in relation to relating with others, such as their clients in therapy.

The ability of secure therapists to recognise what they bring into therapy reflects the conceptual frameworks for understanding family attachments, as discussed by Byng-Hall (2008), in that a secure family base enables individuals to explore their relationships with family members and with outsiders. The capacity to collaborate is higher in individuals with a secure family base where they feel safe to explore new relationships.

Additionally, the secure therapists in the illustrations who experienced challenges were able to be reflexive and process those experiences. This complements the notion of reflexivity proposed by Fonagy et al. (1991, Fonagy and Target, 1997) in that one could overcome the negative impact of adversity with support and the ability to reflect and make sense of those experiences. They found that mental states in oneself and others are developed through observing parents' mental states, where the parents' ability to respond to the child or sensitive caregiving 'provides the psychosocial basis for acquiring and understanding of mind' (p. 691).

Interestingly, they explained that, with a secure attachment style, the mental state of the sensitive caregivers provides a safe space for the child to build in her or his mind the image of the caregiver as evoked by beliefs, feelings, and intentions, and provides a link between the mental state and action. Thus, this explains the ability of secure therapists to reflect on their past struggles and use those experiences to aid their therapeutic work.

What about therapists with 'preoccupied' attachment styles? When Di was asked whether her personal experience helped in her work or personal life, she described an overlap between her own personal experience and her view about her work. She reported difficulty when unable to make the connection between her clients' cases and her own life experiences compared to dealing with cases that were similar to her life path, as described in the excerpt below:

I: So, you feel it (personal experience) helps you in terms of work as well as personal life, the work?

Di: mm both. Coz I think you always think about that stuff, don't you? Or I do, I can't not think about it. You know, when I think about my own family, just about with anything, you can always see something of someone or somewhere, can't you? But it's very rare, and in cases where I really can't see anything, I find the most difficult. Yeah.

Nonetheless, Di illustrated how her personal experience helped her to frame a client's situation in a different light and helped her reflecting team[1] to have a different perspective of the issue. She described disclosing to her team the similarity of her personal experience to her clients. Using her past experience to 'illuminate' clients' difficulties suggests how she used her experience to help the therapeutic process.

But, unlike those with secure attachment styles, Di seemed unsure. She took a long pause and later stated that one could not argue with her experience as it is her truth. Her reaction seemed quite superficial or 'distant'. Even though she talked about using her experience to assist the therapeutic work, Di did not manage to elaborate how she used her personal experience, having a 'strict dad and a sister with mental health problems,' in dealing with clients. When asked whether she thought her experience was helpful, Di was 'preoccupied' with her own issues ('... and I think just they couldn't argue with my experience ...') and appeared to lack empathy as she was focusing more on herself:

Di: You know when I was being part of a reflecting team, I've described difficulties in my own family of origin because I find they may illuminate something for the family that you know, not all the time, but I do remember one situation [when I] really talked about my dad. There was a situation where a girl, questionably sort of psychotic, very suicidal, and a dad who appeared very controlling and I talked about my own family where my dad, when we were young, was really quite strict and (2 secs) and couldn't tolerate very much difference, and my sister who had some (2 secs) you know mental health problems, what that was like actually. You know, I do self-disclose but only something really (silence).

I: helping the process?

Di: well, you hope it would be. You never know do you if something is helpful.

I: the one that you described, was it helpful?

Di: I think it was. Yeah. I think it showed something else that hadn't been ... (10 secs), it showed something else that it was difficult for the parents to understand the girl's difficulty. And I think just they couldn't argue with my experience. They could say it wasn't like that in their family. What I'm saying [is] this is true for me, you can't argue with that, as such can you? You don't know, I hope so. You never know.

Fran seemed to be aware of how her past experience impacted on her work. However, when probed further, Fran did not elaborate how that awareness guided her therapeutic work. In other words, Fran did not discuss how she dealt with her countertransference when facing clients who evoked memories of her past relationship:

Fran: well ... (pause) the couple I was telling you about, where it took me a bit of time to engage with the wife ... mmm (pause) because I had a divorce before and my previous husband was in medicine and these people were both in medicine and I found, and also, strangely enough, I ... my experience was more similar to the man than the woman in question and I did identify with him quite strongly, yes ... yes ...

I: Do you think that affects you in relating to the woman?

Fran: aaaaaaaa (long pause)

I: probably because you identify more with the man

Fran: I think probably a bit, I'd to be careful to correct myself and be aware of it ... it was important that I was aware of that.

The link between personal relationship experience and work as a therapist was also illustrated by 'fearful' therapists (Izzy and Joan) in describing their personal experiences and how that impacted on their work as therapists. Those in the secure attachment styles were able to explain how their personal experiences guide their therapeutic work (as shown by Andy, Betty, and Carl). This, however, was different to their counterparts in the fearful category. Although participating therapists in the fearful category managed to describe their personal experiences, they did not discuss how their past experiences enhanced or hindered the therapeutic process. Izzy, rather, very slowly and subtly stated that the fact that she grew up in a disjointed family, without much communication, influenced her work with families:

> 'Mm, I mean, (3 secs) working with families and thinking about the power of communication that I would have wanted to have myself when I was growing up. So, in that sense, it influences my thinking about more this is how I want to work with families.'
>
> (Izzy)

Izzy had to be probed a few times regarding this, but her answers did not clearly reflect the link between her past experience and her work as a therapist. This is illustrated in the excerpt below:

I: Can you describe, I know this is a bit intrusive, you can say no. When you talked about the influence from your own personal communication in your personal life, what was that influence, to be exact, that has made you decide?

Izzy: ... (12 secs) Well, there's two things. One is as an adult communicating with people and being interested in what makes things better, yeah and the influence ... (6 secs) of my background was about what could have made things better but didn't and therefore looking for that in my work with families. Does that make sense?

I: Yeah, makes sense. You were talking about how your background shaped your work.

Izzy: Yeah, in a way it didn't, it didn't shape me until I did the training, you know it happened then.

Similarly, Joan described her work with a young client and how her personal experience impacted on her work as a family therapist. Although she did not describe how she responded to the client, from the excerpt

I could draw the conclusion that her past experience played a role in her attempts to understand the client's problem:

> 'Her personality, yeah, personality, there is a connection. What's that about? (slow) Maybe it's about me being able to understand what a 17 year old is going through. When I've said, you know, the very first thing that I said when you asked me questions was my father died when I was 17 and I don't know what that was about (very slow again).'
>
> (Joan)

Joan described being aware of her past and talked about the impact it had on her work but did not provide further elaboration on how this helped her respond to clients. This was illustrated as follows:

I: Going back to when you talked about bereavement in your own experience, sometimes we come to cases that are, sort of, similar to our own life stories, so does that, do you think, impact your work as a therapist and how do you deal with that?

Joan: How do I deal with it? Mm ... (12 secs) I'm aware of it and I will talk about it.

This was a much more superficial answer than that given by Betty, who went further in describing how her past led her to think of the steps she needed to take when facing clients with issues that reminded her of her past, stating:

> 'I wouldn't immediately say, oh my mother died too. So, I might think okay, how did you all respond after that? How did your father react? Was he somebody who could show his grief? So, I might be processing my own experience but more to structure the questions.'
>
> (Betty)

The differences between Betty's (secure) and Joan's (fearful) answers illustrate the difference in the depth of answers.

For participating therapists in the dismissing category, there was no clear pattern in their descriptions of the impact of their personal experience on their work as a therapist. For example, let us take a look at

George who described growing up in a 'chaotic' environment. Unlike those in the secure and preoccupied styles, he did not relate his personal experience directly to his work as a therapist, but one gets the impression that the chaos he described had provided him with an insight into a lot of issues, such as couples screaming at each other and being a child in a dysfunctional family. However, it was interesting that he presented familiarity with this 'chaotic, angry and destructive environment' when dealing with such clients' situations but described not feeling bothered or upset, which suggests the dismissing attachment styles of being avoidant and less anxious of abandonment:

> 'I, my family history, my, my family, my immediate family (7 secs) was quite chaotic, and angry and destructive. So, in a sense, when I'm in a mess, I feel I'm on familiar ground. When couples are screaming at each other, I'm not really bothered. Yeah, when there's a lot of emotion, I'm not really upset. And when kids are involved and they're suffering, I'm a parent myself, that I find much more difficult to take. It stirs up quite a lot of stuff for me and I guess, also, because I was a child and there's, sort of, a bit of rather dysfunctional family, I'd rather put it that way but that has helped me, in a way, because I think, the therapy [suggesting the therapeutic work as a two-way process where the therapist also personally benefits from the process] has helped me. I think what has helped me a great deal is, I can now go home to my wife and kids and this sort of balances out.'
>
> (George)

Can you see the differences in the therapists' accounts provided in the examples?

From the excerpts, the secure therapists (Andy, Betty, and Carl) explained the connection between their personal relationship experiences and their therapeutic work. They were able to put their personal experiences into a theoretical perspective and used them to develop their therapeutic work. This was different to their counterparts in the insecure attachment categories.

Although participating therapists with preoccupied attachment styles (Di, Fran) discussed their personal relationships and their work as therapists, they depicted more preoccupation with their own relationships and less discussion of how their personal experiences affected their work. This presentation was also found among the therapists with fearful attachment styles (Izzy, Joan). They did not provide an elaboration concerning how their past experiences shaped their therapeutic work. In other words, the depth of discussion was poles apart between the secure and insecure therapists in this study.

The stories narrated by participating therapists in the study show that therapists' positive past experiences – the ability to process past challenges and reflect on them – as displayed by the secure therapists, enabled them to be more 'available' to their clients. Interestingly, Hersoug et al. (2001), in their study on the quality of working alliance in psychotherapy, reported a positive association between therapists' memories of past relationships, such as a caring mother, and their evaluation of the quality of working alliance. A positive past experience acts as a buffer to the challenges faced by therapists in their work. Additionally, in their study, Leiper and Casares (2000) showed that insecure psychologists experience more difficulty in their therapeutic work and feel that their work life interferes with their personal life. The insecure therapists are less able to draw on the 'self', i.e., their personal experience, in therapeutic work. Does this mean that therapists' negative experiences are unhelpful in their work as therapists?

The therapists' accounts suggest that attachment styles and experience, especially the combination of positive experiences and secure attachment styles, assist therapists in their work, as illustrated by Carl, with a complaining mother, who knows his limits and understands the impact of his experience on his therapeutic work. Nevertheless, the type of experience is less important as compared to having a secure attachment style. So, it is not so much the type of experience that matters. You can have a negative experience like the death of a family member and still be able to process the experience and acknowledge the impact of such an experience on your work, as shown by the examples provided by the secure therapists. Ward (2010) explained that the extent to which we are able to acknowledge and work at understanding our experiences is more important than the type of experience – positive or negative – that we have to face. He suggested that therapists need to process their experiences and understand how these experiences may resonate in the present. How do we do this? We can do this through training and supervision, as described by the participants in Chapter 5.

Chapter summary

- The influences of one's decision to become a therapist or counsellor depend on various factors, among others, family history and good role models.
- This chapter describes the idea that the therapist is able to be an internal observer to his/her past challenges.
- Therapists' voices show the impact of family of origin, critical incidents, and personal experiences in the work of therapists.
- The interviews illustrated differences in therapists' presentations based on their attachment styles. Therapists with secure attachment styles illustrated the ability to put their personal experiences into perspectives and used them to guide their work.

Note

1 A reflecting team is a process involving a team of supportive professionals, who collaborate with the client to offer multiple perspectives. It involves dialogue, the use of a one-way mirror, and feedback.

5

The Relationship between Attachment Styles and Alliance: Therapists' Stories

This chapter focuses on

- the relationship of attachment and becoming a therapist;
- therapists' views on therapeutic alliance in engagement within the therapeutic system;
- what therapists said in terms of emotional connection within the therapeutic system;
- safety within the therapeutic system; and
- therapists' contributions to a shared sense of purpose within the family.

Therapeutic alliance: from the lens of the therapists

The self of the therapist is the most important tool that a therapist brings into therapy. The therapist must be able to provide appropriate responses, which often must be done on the spot. Notwithstanding all the skills that a therapist has mastered from his or her training and practice, they are not enough to make a 'good' therapist. The attachment theory proposes that reflexivity allows an individual to reflect upon the actions of others as well as those of oneself that impact on a relationship. This requires an ongoing introspection on the part of the therapist as to what might work or not work in therapy, which includes the therapist's own bias and limitations. A 'secure' attachment style is essential for us to look deeper within ourselves and to become a 'secure base' for our clients.

Therapeutic alliance – the research

For the qualitative in-depth semi-structured interviews, 13 family therapists were asked to bring in a case and reflect upon the case and answer questions related to alliance building. The interview guide was built based on the System for Observing Family Therapy Alliances (SOFTA).

All four dimensions of therapeutic alliance were discussed by the therapists in the interviews. For this theme, what therapists stated was presented according to the four alliance dimensions (based on the SOFTA template) and their attachment styles. Therapists in the study discussed all four dimensions of therapeutic alliance based on SOFTA: the engagement within the therapeutic system, emotional connection with the therapist, safety within the therapeutic system, and shared sense of purpose within the family. However, the last two dimensions of the therapeutic alliance reflected differences in the therapists' views according to their attachment styles. This probably related to the therapists' roles in providing a secure attachment and a safe space; as discussed by Bowlby (1988a) in his five therapeutic tenets and Byng-Hall's (1995) idea of therapists providing a 'temporary secure base' for families in therapy (Byng-Hall, 1995, p. 6).

Key Points 5.1

- This suggests a relationship between the therapists' attachment styles and their ability to provide an emotional connection within the therapeutic system as well as safety within the therapeutic system.
- On the other hand, 'engagement within the therapeutic system' and 'shared sense of purpose within the family' did not show any differences, probably because these dimensions did not evoke any 'attachment related feelings' as they were more directed towards the clients or therapy in general.

Engagement within the therapeutic system

Therapists explained what they did to engage clients in therapy, particularly those they considered 'difficult' or 'quiet'. Let us look at the evidence of whether there are differences associated with therapists' attachment styles based on the therapists' responses below:

Therapy as a Collaborative Decision-Making Process

Asking clients what they wanted to discuss or what they wanted in therapy was part of the way the therapists engaged the family members in therapy. Therapy was described as a 'collaborative' process by Izzy, who stated:

> 'I think that's a little bit about collaboration. It's not me who sets all the rules and the guidelines. Maybe sometimes there isn't … (4 secs) a clarity and maybe that's because you don't know how it's going to go. Some of it is aa, you know, like session to session, so who should we invite to the next session? Who is it going to be useful for? What does the young person want, particularly?'
>
> (Izzy)

In a similar example, Donna illustrated how she asked reluctant clients what they wanted to do, and, in doing so, she was giving the clients a choice to be involved in making the decision to stay in therapy, as described in the excerpt below:

> 'I would say okay, now what do you want to do? Do you want to come back? So, it's like turning it over to them and giving the power back to them. Because if they're here under duress, they usually won't engage, but if you somehow find a way, put them in charge of it that they can make the decision or make it sound like if they experienced feeling accepted and heard and the conversation is positive, very often they say yeah okay I'll come back and then you got them. And then they'll engage, and they'll stay with you.'
>
> (Donna)

To conclude, in engaging the client as a collaborative process, when George was asked how he explained to clients how therapy works, he stated that it depended on how specific he wanted to be. He also explained that the first few sessions were more about getting to know the clients, to see whether they fit the notion of the 'chemistry between the client – therapist' relationship. As illustrated by George, here:

> 'That's an interesting question. I think it depends on the context. If I'm working, well it doesn't actually depend on the context. But depends on the context in how specific I am. And what approach I'm trying to take. So, if I'm working systemically, if I'm working more humanistically than cognitively than I tend to do much more explanation than if I'm working more…(tut tu tut tu, he muttered trying to find words) if I think it's useful to work in a sort of transparent manner. But, I guess, I tend to think, anyway, the first couple of sessions, are sort of an assessment process and I think of assessment as a two-way process. They get to know me, if they want to work with me and I get to see whether I can work with them, with the family, with the individual or everybody.'
>
> (George)

Exercise 5.1 Compare and Describe

- Can you see the differences based on the examples above?
- Describe what you observed based on the given examples.

As suggested by the examples above, there were no differences associated with the therapists' different attachment styles. The therapists, regardless of attachment style, discussed the two-way communications involved in therapeutic work. They described the importance of being transparent and allowing clients to judge the fit between the therapist-client relationships before embarking on therapeutic work.

Engaging Difficult Clients or Situations

The therapists have worked with many types of clients, and, in engagement within the therapeutic system, the therapists described things they did to engage difficult or quiet clients as well as to tackle difficult situations.

For example, Eleanor described the importance of stopping a family member from dominating the session, in order to provide another member of the family a chance to voice his or her opinion. This allowed the therapist to engage with the quiet or less dominant client, as explained in the excerpt below:

> 'He (the husband) tends to talk for his wife quite a lot and English is her second language so, in the first place, it was easier to engage with him because he's the one speaking for them so what makes the difference, I think, was two things. One: me kind of almost stopping him in his tracks, saying it's really important for me to listen to his wife and kind of affirming the fact that there could be, that it was quite okay for them to have different opinions and mm, so I think that helped her to then feel she could have a voice and that would help my engagement with her.'
>
> (Eleanor)

Betty said that engaging a reluctant family needs to be done slowly, as well as persistently:

> 'I think my style with a reluctant family would be to try and respond to when they want to be seen; to take the issues as they come up; but to take them slowly but to keep mentioning them, to never stop mentioning them but find ways that fit with this family ...'
>
> (Betty)

A similar strategy was also used by Di, who stated that she moved back and forth between things that were easy to talk about and more difficult topics:

> 'I try to move from the thing that was easy to talk about to more difficult, you know sort of dancing back and forth.'
>
> (Di)

In summary, engaging difficult clients and situations required the therapists to be persistent in a very respectful way, where they described gradually approaching the clients, allowing clients to try them out, and offering a lot of appointments. From the illustrations, there was no difference between therapists' attachment styles and engaging difficult clients or situations.

Emotional Connection within the Therapeutic System

Most therapists in this study disclosed their personal reactions or feelings towards their clients or the situation at hand. They expressed empathy for their clients' struggle, and they explained their views regarding self-disclosure. Let us look at whether therapists differed in some of the ways they emotionally connected to clients according to their attachment styles.

Therapists Express Empathy for the Clients' Struggle

Empathy is an understanding of the experience of another person. The therapist's ability to convey the message that he or she understands the experience of the client (Friedlander et al., 2005) is captured in this category.

Secure therapists in this study (Betty and Carl) described acknowledging clients' struggles. Betty empathised with her clients, and she also acknowledged the feelings involved in such situations. She showed that she understood her clients' feelings by acknowledging the situation, as well as her own reaction towards the situation:

> 'I would always tend to hold on to my tears but if I sort of felt, actually, this is part of what we were talking about, I might say look when I'm talking to people and really sad that things have happened, my eyes swell up like this. It's not because what you're saying I don't want to hear. I hate you to think I wasn't human. What you're saying is really sad. So, I'll tend to sort of acknowledge my sadness but I try and do it after we've had the chance to acknowledge theirs. So, I might say to them is talking about this topic, is this okay, and if somebody then starts to cry, I will say but it's interesting because I was thinking what you were saying.'
>
> (Betty)

Similarly, Carl, when asked what he would do when facing a difficult situation and trying to make clients open up in the session, stated that he would acknowledge the feelings involved. He also commented that it would be a mistake to ignore the feelings that arose in the session. The two examples illustrate the importance of acknowledging the clients' feelings as well as the therapists' feelings, to convey an understanding of the clients' point of view and to be able to respond to clients' vulnerability:

> 'I try to acknowledge it. Often you can tell if people are angry. I think it's a mistake to ignore that all and carry on. Often a teenager's scowling and I say

'I get the feeling this is not your favourite place to be today, that's alright, I understand that. Why would you want to come here?' So, just acknowledging, that I don't mind ... I'm not put off by people not liking me, being angry with me, and to try to be interested in understanding their point of views and then I think people then will be engaged, will feel safe.'

(Carl)

Key Points 5.2

- There were no differences in the way that the participating family therapists with 'insecure' attachment styles ('preoccupied/dismissing and fearful') presented when faced with situations that needed the therapists to convey understanding towards their clients' struggle.
- For those in the secure attachment style, three different aspects were visible when conveying empathy towards clients: 1) acknowledging the clients' feelings, 2) acknowledging their own feelings, and 3) conveying understanding of the clients' point of view and being able to respond to clients' vulnerability.

For example, Andy summed up clearly how having a secure attachment helps to foster good relationships. He showed awareness of, and empathy for, the vicious cycle (rejection and wanting to be accepted) that was often presented in the families that he had worked with:

'I think because, previously, I worked with children in a [children's social] care team. It convinced me, really, maybe it's personality, but maybe it's the quality of attachment that they have had with their parents and so on and therefore that determines how they attach to their children and to other people as well. If you've got that secure attachment you are more able, perhaps, to manage your emotions because, if you show those emotions, nobody's going to reject you. But lots of people's experience, since I've been working here looking at the families and parents' backgrounds and their relationship to their parents, sometimes, there's that theme – If you show your emotions, people reject or they leave or sometimes there's disruptions in your childhood where significant individuals had left the family.'

(Andy)

A similar presentation could be seen with participating therapists with insecure attachment styles, where they acknowledged their clients' feelings, but most of them did not acknowledge their own feelings when facing such situations, as illustrated below. The therapists described waiting for the right moment to convey their understanding of clients' situations to avoid paralysing the therapeutic process. Unlike their secure counterparts, none of the therapists in the insecure attachment styles described that they would acknowledge their own feelings in conveying empathy towards their clients.

For example, Eleanor explained how she showed her understanding by acknowledging the client's difficulty and empathising with her situation:

> '… the mum was talking about how difficult it was when she'd been having this quality time with her daughter and then she had to get on and do the jobs, in the household, make the tea or whatever and then the daughter was cross and wanted her attention. So, then I, sort of, talked a little bit about how difficult it is to split yourself in two when you've got to be doing jobs and so, I think, I don't think I actually said that for young children, but I, sort of, showed my understanding of how I understood the issues that she was talking about.'
>
> (Eleanor)

Similarly, Di talked about acknowledging the client's difficulty. However, she did not provide any further explanation:

> 'So, it, sort of, acknowledging what we're talking about was very difficult, was very difficult stuff. Yeah it was difficult. She was turned away from her mum but she didn't get up and go. You know, she's the girl that absconded, she's got it in her to aa …'
>
> (Di)

Ken described the need to wait for the right moment in order to acknowledge the client's feelings. Once that acknowledgement had been made, he would seek the client's permission before continuing the process:

> 'So, I guess, kind of, you know, waiting, waiting for a moment when it feels appropriate to offer something like a tissue but also acknowledging that

they might be upset, and you know checking with them if it's ok to carry on because sometimes they'd be quite distressed.'

(Ken)

However, he also acknowledged that there were times when clients' experiences were completely beyond his experience, but it still created an impact, and that, to him, meant empathy. Nonetheless, Ken did not discuss how he would handle such situations with his clients besides going to his colleagues for 'support'. There was no element of acknowledging the clients' difficult experiences in his illustration:

'But I don't think that always has to be the case because, I mean, you know, sometimes you heard something and it's completely out of your experience but … (3 secs) what they went through still has a resonance for you. Sorry, sometimes it's where, you know, we would have cases where we probably go and talk to a colleague and say you couldn't make that up could you. Sometimes it's so out of our experience. There was a, kind of, almost a shock element. It just can't be imagined. That creates empathy as well.'

(Ken)

Additionally, one also gets the sense that the response should be structured in order that clients are not paralysed by the situation. The problem should be responded to with compassion (with an acknowledgement and the offering of a tissue), before moving on to the next level:

'I guess it's, ultimately, to be attentive to that. I notice it by, you know, by having tissues, by offering compassion, things like that but not to be so organised by that level of distress that it paralyses the process of therapy. So, to be organised and attentive to it sufficiently.'

(George)

Fran illustrated how she attended when clients showed their vulnerability in her session. From her description, I concluded that she was emotionally 'detached' from the situation. Her explanation was similar to that given by George, who provided tissues, and acknowledged the challenges that clients were facing. However, she did not provide any further explanation. It felt very 'cold' – not very empathic, with no acknowledgement of her own feelings and what she would do to help clients:

I: When clients show vulnerability in a session, they discuss painful feelings, or they cry in the session, do you attend to that?

Fran: Yes ... I always give them some tissues, I say 'it's upsetting, isn't it? It's very distressing', yeah.

I: Usually when you do that, what kind of reaction do you get from the clients?

Fran: Usually, they just use the tissues.

Donna's secure attachment style on the ECR was incongruent with her behaviour in the interview; her presentation was similar to those in the insecure category. Throughout the interview, she repeatedly stressed her 'love for clients' ('I think I just have a great love for the clients. I do actually love them, I care a lot about them, you have to love them in a sense of wishing well towards them'). She explained how she reassured her clients or normalised her clients' feelings. She conveyed understanding, but the excerpt also suggests the significance of her own 'needs', that she wants the clients to know that she respects and loves them:

> 'And, of course, I assured her that I heard several things before and nothing shocked me. I said you couldn't shock me, you couldn't disappoint me. I still respect you, I still love you. Then I assured her, you're innocent, you were a child, you didn't do anything wrong, you've nothing to be ashamed of.'
>
> (Donna)

Thus, with regard to expressing empathy for the clients' struggle, the therapists with secure attachment styles acknowledged their clients' feelings, and acknowledged their own reactions or struggles, while managing to empathise with their clients' difficulty. The therapists with insecure attachment styles, on the other hand, empathised but did not display their feelings. It seems as if the therapists with insecure attachment styles were 'detached', where the gap in the therapist – client's relationship was much wider, that is, 'I'm the therapist, they are the client.'

Self-disclosure

Most therapists that I interviewed, regardless of their attachment styles, agreed with the use of self-disclosure to enhance the therapeutic process, or, if it is deemed necessary, to promote client care. There were relatively small differences between therapists with secure and insecure attachment styles concerning self-disclosure, which could be noted in terms of the 'depth' of the therapists' views and how they used self-disclosure in their own work. The analysis is divided according to secure and insecure attachment styles and therapists' agreement or disagreement on the subject matter.

Three secure therapists said they would self-disclose if it would benefit the therapeutic process.

Andy described the feeling of awkwardness when he had to disclose that he did not have children during his early days of becoming a therapist, as illustrated below:

> Andy: I used, I used to feel quite awkward when I didn't have children, I was doing this job. Families would say 'have you got kids?' And I said 'no … actually no' … so there was that fraud feeling – How can you be sitting there and telling me about children when you don't have any.
>
> I: How did you address that?
>
> Andy: I used to address it by saying, 'but I've worked with lots of children in similar situations', but now I've got children. I think I would be able to share with clients that my children aren't perfect …

Betty and Carl gave slightly different opinions to this. Betty stated that she would be cautious of using too much self-disclosure. Betty's concern was more about the meaning of what she might represent to her clients:

> 'I would. I do, but I would tend to use it much more as a story, so I would say something like, I had a family and they were telling me this. I had another family that told me that … I think I'd be cautious at using too much personal self-disclosure more because I'm interested in the meaning I have for families …'
>
> (Betty)

This response was similar to Carl, whose concern was about the meaning that self-disclosure might have for his clients. Carl added that self-disclosure might have a negative outcome and create more distance if clients perceived the therapist as someone that they could not relate to:

> 'What can he possibly understand about us … he obviously comes from a nice middle-class family, and so actually seems to create more distance rather than a sense of connection. It's as if the therapist does not really get it, they think oo … that therapist thinks he can understand us, he doesn't really. So, I found that actually, if you say it, if you self-disclose, it can seem to close things down a little bit. That's the danger of it. But it can work fine, but I feel, often, it has these other consequences …'
>
> (Carl)

Carl did not reject the idea of self-disclosure. However, he did not think that self-disclosure was always helpful:

> 'Well I think, actually, do I need to know about this man, you know … who is this about here? So often people like to think the therapist, sort of, like, an idealised figure to start with, and they need that … Later on, perhaps, it can begin to diminish … So, it's not that I'm against self-disclosure, I just don't … I just don't feel that it is always as helpful and sometimes, in particular, family therapists tend to think it's quite helpful.'
>
> (Carl)

Donna described how she rarely self-disclosed. She did not oppose the idea, but when asked to elaborate, explained that she did not want clients to know too much about her. Even though it was not directly highlighted, the issue of the boundary in the therapist – client relationship was raised, and she expressed concern about being too open with the clients:

> 'Rarely … rarely. There are people who have a big taboo and wouldn't tell their clients anything about themselves. I wouldn't be as rigid as that. But I rarely tell them anything personal about myself. I tell them things that I know would genuinely help them.
>
> I don't want the client to know too much about me, because I think that's not what it's about. Then they start to be more interested in me than you are in them and I imagine they would. And they imagine I'm their friend that's got to tell them things or that I'm going to tell them things and they are going to tell me, and I don't want that kind of relationship with them. So, no, I rarely tell them but if it would help them, I would tell them.'
>
> (Donna)

Lin neither agreed nor disagreed regarding self-disclosure. She described how she had partially disclosed her private life to clients through public domains, such as in a book she had written and on her website:

> 'Some of them would already know because it's got to be online somewhere. They get it from the website. It doesn't say that I mention my book so many times, but it does say that I'm a mother. So, this is, kind of, like, in a public domain. Everybody who Googles me will find it so I see no point in hiding it but then they may ask how old you are and I would basically answer with a question, "is there a particular reason you need to know?" The whole business of self-disclosure ...'
>
> (Lin)

However, on a different occasion, Lin described how she would self-disclose depending on the situation; nevertheless, the material she suggested self-disclosing was non emotional. This seemed to be similar to the process of this interview where she appeared to be reluctant to discuss emotionally related materials:

> Lin: Well depends what, what it is. Just by being here, I already self-disclose where I live, and they can probably go to Google and see how much I pay for the house.
>
> I: (laugh)
>
> Lin: It's true. [serious tone]
>
> I: Ok yeah.
>
> Lin: That's how it works. So, if I self-disclose it's a question of who is it serving, in my opinion. I would never say something voluntarily about my family unless I really thought that it could help people and that I would say one in 20 people, no probably 2% of my clients I would say something personal about myself, voluntarily.

For the 'preoccupied' therapists (Eleanor, Di, and Fran), self-disclosure should not take away from the main focus – clients' issues – and should be done according to the situation. For example, Fran reported that she would self-disclose about 'her professional experience'. Fran explained that self-disclosure depended on the length of the therapeutic work, whether she had known the family long enough, and whether clients have shown progress in therapy. However, she admitted that she did not usually disclose her personal experiences:

I: Have you used self-disclosure throughout your years of experience?

Fran: mmm … yes … I do say, I mean, today, it's the question the couple I see and whether they are going to bring their son. I said in my experience it can be useful, so I said that yes … but it's actually my professional experience not my personal experience.

I: What about your personal experience?

Fran: aa … not usually … not usually, no.

I: Are you against it, totally or (cut by Fran)

Fran: No, I'm not, no … I think it depends how far you are on in your therapy. I mean, I have one family finished about a year and a half ago and I've known them for two years, I think. So, that … mm, I'm more, then I think I did then tell them that I've got a big step-family but it wouldn't be until I've known them very well and they were virtually alright, they've got better.

In terms of participating therapists with 'dismissing' attachment styles, neither Harry nor George fully subscribed to the idea of self-disclosure. On three different occasions, Harry explained his views regarding self-disclosure. When asked whether he thought it is alright to self-disclose, Harry took quite a while to answer the question, and he then stated that it was fine to self-disclose if it was within limits ('It's a tough question to answer … I would say, I would say mm I think self-disclosure within limits is fine'). Harry explained that he would be interested in knowing why clients wanted to find out about him.

His view regarding the subject matter was illuminated when he explained his position in that he was not keen on the idea of self-disclosure as it might impact on the client's own self-disclosure in therapy, which might create a boundary, as illustrated in the excerpts below:

> 'I think I've knowledge of what it's like for me, but I think there's been certain bits of information that you can disclose about yourself which lessen or, possibly, impact on the disclosure that the people you're in conversation with. You know, they would kind of put a boundary about themselves or something like

that. For instance, if I was sexually abused as a child, then how on earth would that be helpful? You know.'

(Harry)

Similarly, George, in his own words, tended to 'shy away' from self-disclosure when working with families. There was some similarity in the way the two therapists described their views on the subject matter. Harry's concern was about the impact of self-disclosure and the boundary that it might create within the therapeutic relationship, while George's comments illustrated that because of pressures families face in society, self-disclosing himself might further exacerbate the notion that the family has to fit into his (the therapist's) norms or ideas. Though it was not highlighted directly, his comments suggest the 'boundary' that self-disclosure might impose on clients:

George: I tend not to with families. Maybe with individuals, a bit, when it's really appropriate. But not particularly with families because, why do I not with families? Because I think ... (4 secs), I think there's enough pressure with families traditionally to subscribe to some norms to think in with some sort of cultural norms and the last thing they need is to try to fit with Therapist X's norms. To try to be the type of parents or couple or whatever that I think they should be.

I: So, you use less self-disclosure?

George: I think I use less self-disclosure. Having said that, of course, in therapy there is self-disclosure because if they mentioned something that's frightening, and I say oh, that might have been quite frightening. I'm disclosing that I found it frightening. I tend to shy away from that when working with families.

(George)

Key Points 5.3

There were similarities in therapists with insecure attachment styles ('preoccupied', 'dismissing', and 'fearful') regarding self-disclosure. They generally reported two specific issues related to self-disclosure:

- It should not take away from the main focus and depends on how well the therapist knows the family (Fran, Eleanor, and Izzy).

- It should be within limits (safe, general, not an emotional experience; as described by Fran, Di, Joan, and Harry). Even though therapist Harry described the use of self-disclosure within limits, 'dismissing' therapists in this study tend to shy away from using self-disclosure in their practices (George and Harry).

Despite the similarities, the ways in which the therapists voiced their opinions were different. Those in the preoccupied category generally did not reject the idea of self-disclosure but limited its use, while their counterparts in the dismissing category tended to shy away from self-disclosure. In contrast, participating therapists with fearful attachment styles described more acceptance in the use of self-disclosure, as described by Izzy and Joan. Neither of them had objections or concerns regarding the use of self-disclosure in their work. To illustrate, Joan described the use of a third person's experience as an example to clients, instead of using a direct self-exposure:

> 'I do use self-disclosure but, maybe, I would say I know somebody who has this experience or people that I see here generally tell me, so it wouldn't be direct self-exposure. Sometimes it might be with parents when it's not such an emotional experience.'
>
> (Joan)

Key Points 5.4

- There were mixed views regarding self-disclosure, with most therapists willing to self-disclose if they believed it would help the therapeutic process.
- However, there were differences in the degree of the participating therapists' reflections in choosing when self-disclosure was appropriate. Secure therapists, like Andy and Betty, would use self-disclosure to foster an emotional connection and alliance. Carl (secure) questioned whether self-disclosure would be helpful in fostering alliance, although he did not totally reject the idea of self-disclosure. This participant considered that self-disclosure did not necessarily have to be verbalised because responding empathetically towards clients could also constitute disclosure.
- The secure therapists' discussions reflected Friedlander et al.'s (2006) opinion that clients are attracted to therapists who speak from their personal experience, thus enhancing engagement. Additionally, having a similar background or experience gave these therapists the ability to be empathic, and, though unspoken, self-disclosure was visible through the therapist's behaviour that conveyed understanding.

Key Points 5.5

- The insecure therapists provided mixed views. Most would self-disclose, when necessary, but some were merely responding to clients' questions instead of self-disclosing (e.g., George) in order to foster an emotional connection and alliance.
- Insecure therapists in this study described disclosing in relation to 'normal' or trivial, impersonal matters which focused more on their professional capacity.
- The therapists' lack of self-disclosure may be associated with their preferred therapeutic model. Dismissing therapists (George and Harry) preferred the Milan-Systemic and Psychoanalytic approaches; neither model subscribes to the idea of self-disclosure. Conversely, it could also be that these therapists shy away from the idea of self-disclosure and choose these therapeutic models accordingly.

Self-disclosure can be helpful if it does not redirect the session to focus on the therapist's issues. Thus, therapists need to be mindful when to self-disclose and be aware of the purpose of such disclosure. Therapists need to always reflect in practice to guide their intentions and ask themselves when self-disclosure might and might not benefit the clients. Self-disclosure when used correctly and in the right situation can be a powerful tool to strengthen the alliance.

Safety within the therapeutic system

The therapists in my study explained their contributions to creating a feeling of safety within the therapeutic system. They discussed providing structure and confidentiality and described their attempts to contain or manage hostility between family members.

Providing structure and confidentiality

All the therapists, regardless of their attachment styles, discussed the way the therapy sessions would unfold (the ground rules and how therapy would be structured). They explained confidentiality procedures and the extent to which information might have to be shared with third parties, such as the social services, and in what circumstances.

Overall, the therapists did not differ in their views regarding providing structure to the sessions and ensuring confidentiality.

Therapists' views about containing or managing clients' hostility

Many of the therapists described managing clients' hostility or difficult situations as a 'balancing act'. They attempted to control or manage clients' hostility or a difficult situation in various and differing ways.

Fran indicated that she would acknowledge her clients' strong feelings and usually that would help to keep the therapy moving; as illustrated below:

> 'Well, in that situation I usually acknowledge it. "I can see you're very angry", or "you're very upset" or "it's very distressing" and I find that, once their emotion has been acknowledged, that very often, that's enough to get the therapy moving on again.'
>
> (Fran)

Betty illustrated how, when facing clients who were more dominant, or who were angry, she would take control by calming the situation, and reasoning with clients, telling them that part of family therapy is about listening to differences:

> 'If one is more dominant, I've various little phrases, you know. I'll say things like "it sounds like you are really keen, I understand probably would it be okay if I get you to tell me your bit and then just ask you to hold on for a minute". Because part of family therapy is hearing the differences. So, it's quite important I hear everybody.'
>
> (Betty)

She elaborated that she would try to make clients realise that they are shouting and to reason with them. Betty would use humour to lighten the situation and if things were out of control, she would be firm and use other techniques, such as writing on the whiteboard, to defuse the situation. She explained about playing around with the structure to see what fits or what might work, such as checking how things are:

> 'If they are actually shouting at each other, I will say things like "look, I'm going to have to slow you down there because people in the corridor will get worried, they'll phone security, we really don't need security howling in here". I'll be a bit humorous. But, say it was really serious, I would just stand up and say "look I'm sorry I can't have this. You can express strong views..." or I have to use the whiteboard if it is getting heated. I'll write down dad and his views, son...I might sort of then slow it down and say "can I just stop and check how is this working for people? Is the way we are talking okay? Do we need to do it a bit differently?" And then a young person might say to me, "I'm just getting furious", "Do you want to go and sit behind there (two-way-mirror) and watch?" Or "would you like to talk to somebody separately?" I just play around with it, structurally.'
>
> (Betty)

Finally, Betty asserted that it would be an insight for her team to see what is going on when clients were shouting and were about to leave the session. She stated that it is quite an important time, providing added information that you should not lose by 'wrapping it up' prematurely. In other words, she made a safe space for clients to vent their frustrations but did not let it escalate so that it provided useful information for the therapeutic process:

> 'In some ways, when that's happening [clients' shouting and wanting to leave], it's quite useful for my team to let me know what was going on at that moment when they look as if they were about to leave. Then we can be in quite a crucial area so I wouldn't want to lose it by wrapping it up too quickly, but I also don't want people stomping out. So, it's that fine balance really.'
>
> (Betty)

A conflict sometimes allowed the therapist to get to the underlying problems which otherwise could not be witnessed by the therapist. This was discussed by Andy and Betty, but Eleanor went further by acknowledging the difficulty of handling such a situation. When clients' cooperation is hard to gain, and the therapist does not have much information to work with, the clients' hostility towards each other might provide some clues to the underlying issues that the family is facing. However, Eleanor was struggling with a member of a family and the way she managed was by asking her client to take a break. Nevertheless, there was not much display of her role in handling the situation, unlike secure therapists (Andy and Betty) who put a stop, reasoned, used humour or, in other ways, problem solved in the situation:

> 'Well, that's tricky. The other family that I was talking about, the one where the girl was verbally abusive to her mother, so that's really hard, to know how to deal with that. I mean, I let it run. I let it run for a bit because, actually, when she's shouting at her mother, it's quite informative as to her point of view mm ... (1 sec) because, some other time, she's refusing to answer anything and she sits with you asking stupid questions (tiny laugh) so we were not getting much of her point of view. So, when she's shouting, at least it's more real, you know, mm, but at some point, I've actually said we can't carry on like this, so I've asked for something different to happen. At one time, she went behind the screen for example and another time, because she's an anorexic, I asked for her to be weighed for a little while, just to give a bit of a break so we can come back again and start fresh.'
>
> (Eleanor)

This is very much in tune with Donna who reported that she would show clients how to manage their anger by reminding them that they were shouting and asking them to lower their voices. By doing so, Donna seemed to control the situation:

> 'You show them how to do it, but you also reassure them that you will protect them almost from themselves. "You're shouting, I need you to lower your voice". So, to remind them, to be contained.'
>
> (Donna)

Donna then explained that she would establish some boundaries to contain the conflict from escalating. In her description, she would acknowledge the client's anger ('it's okay to be angry') and not let the situation get out of hand as illustrated below. Unlike other (ECR-defined) secure therapists, Donna did not elaborate on the 'fine balancing act' of wanting to get more information, and, at the same time, trying to manage the situation. She also did not show that she was managing the situation through reasoning, other than providing boundaries that focus on their safety:

> 'I would have had one or two very angry men over the time. But I would very quickly kind of establish some boundaries around that. It's okay to be angry but I must ask you to sit. Well they both have to remain seated for their own safety and once you've contained them and told them you must remain seated, they're fine. I don't mind if they shout. They're just expressing.'
>
> (Donna)

In the event, when faced with a situation where one client seemed to be dominating the session, like his counterparts who had tried to stop the situation from escalating, Harry commented that he would react according to what he noticed. He tried to problem solve the situation with clients when he invited clients to think of ways to allow other family members' voices to be heard in the session. Nonetheless, it was quite odd or strong when he confronted clients and told them that he was more interested in knowing the opinion of another family member.

George clearly disagreed that conflict should be allowed to escalate in the therapeutic process. Although he would not necessarily stop the conflict, he would try to understand the explosion and invite the family to look at the process:

> 'I think you can't allow, you can't seem to be in collusion with parents or whatever mmm … (9 secs) that abused a child. I mean, similarly, I work quite a lot with couples. You can't allow a couple to have a full-blown row in the room. You can, in the sense, but mm it's not, if it's a row it's one thing but clear verbal abuse and intimidation and if you're there and you're neutral, you align yourself, you declare yourself, at least disinterested. So, you know I won't necessarily stop but I would stop and say "listen you're coming here for me to be part of this because you can do this, I'm pretty sure you can do this at home without my presence" so then I would say "let's talk about what's happening here so we can look at the process" but I'm not really ready to allow or to be part of an abusive sort of… situation.'
>
> (George)

George invited clients to discuss the underlying meaning of the explosion. George was also very strong in his approach when he stated that he did not think there was the need to slow things down. Hearing his explanation, I felt that the notion of safety could probably be jeopardised when he pointed out who holds the power in therapy ('I don't think you're paying me or you're coming here for me to witness this type of…') as shown below:

> 'I don't think I need to calm things down…I think we should try to understand it. If there's an explosion in the room, if there's an aggression in the room, I'll say, I'll try to manage it. I'll say, "I don't think you're paying me or you're coming here for me to witness this type of … (6 secs) … but perhaps you needed to show me something so that we can understand this". I try to open it up and pack it up a bit.'
>
> (George)

Managing a conflict, again, was seen as a balancing act by George. However, when a conflict occurs, one should decide whether the work should continue. This is when a conflict is beyond repair, and, in extreme cases, a contract should be drawn up to inform clients that termination would take place if the conflict is not manageable. This suggests that trying to manage a client's conflict involves not merely a decision-making process on the therapist's part but also the client's realisation of what is manageable. By drawing up a contract, the therapist is making the point that intolerable behaviours are not acceptable, and that clients should not abuse the session:

> 'I think, if there is a session where there is huge escalation of conflict, you try to, you manage there and then, and you have to decide whether the work can continue. In extremes, I actually set up a contract with a client saying there would be a sort of termination of therapeutic contract if there is an escalation beyond what is reasonable to manage.'
>
> (George)

Key Points 5.6

From the excerpts discussed, therapists would manage conflict by:

- stopping it from escalating to an unmanageable level,
- trying to take control by calming things down,
- reasoning with clients, and
- allowing clients to realise what had taken place.

From their responses, secure therapists in this study seemed to show that they were better able to manage and provide a safe setting and act as a secure base for their clients compared to the insecure therapists.

> **Key Points 5.7**
>
> The secure therapists illustrated:
>
> - a softer approach; and
> - the use of humour and reasoning as ways to provide safety.
>
> The insecure therapists did either of the following:
>
> - they were very 'strong' in their approach, which almost felt like they were trying to take control of the situation by putting clients in their place and reminding them of who was in charge (George and Harry); or
> - they merely acknowledged the conflict (Fran), focusing more on safety (Donna) or instructing clients to behave differently (Eleanor) but failing to provide any reasons.

Therapy involves taking risks

In the interview, five therapists, no matter what their attachment styles, explained that the therapeutic process involved clients taking risks and discussing private matters. This, however, could not happen if clients did not feel safe in therapy.

Enabling clients to take risks also meant that the therapists acknowledge the difficulty that their clients are facing in discussing their issues. Even though it was not directly highlighted, being sensitive to a client's situation might provide a safe space for clients to explore their issues. In this illustration, Andy exemplified this, understanding his clients' anxieties, and respecting their right to voice what they want and not to feel coerced into doing so:

> 'I think I've said, sometimes, with people I, sort of, pre-empted some of their anxieties and said "we don't have to talk about anything you don't want to

> talk about, but it would help me if I can ask a few questions about something difficult like domestic violence, is that ok? You don't have to describe exactly what happened, but I would be interested in whatever". By asking. Giving them permission not to give me all the details.'
>
> (Andy)

Eleanor explained that it was not always safe for people to share their concerns in family therapy. For example, she tried to create a safe context for her young client to disclose her sexuality to her father, but things did not work out for her client as the risks were probably too much to bear:

> 'I think, inevitably, it isn't always safe for people to share what's really going on … I was trying to create a safe context so she could open up but actually because her dad was finding it all so difficult, was finding the whole business of talking to be very outside of his usual way of relating to his daughter. I think, because he finds it so uncomfortable, it wasn't very safe for her to share and to talk to him and to feel supported by him and they didn't come back. So, you know, although I do try to make things feel safe, sometimes in families it isn't safe to say what's really going on so I think you can only do this to a certain amount.'
>
> (Eleanor)

Fran seemed unsure when asked whether therapy involved taking risks. She was focusing more on the risk that she was taking rather than that of the clients:

> I: Do you acknowledge that therapy involves taking risk?
>
> Fran: No.
>
> I: In terms of clients?
>
> Fran: You mean to myself or … or them?
>
> I: Both.
>
> Fran: No. I … I … acknowledge to myself that I'm taking a risk.
>
> I: In what sense?
>
> Fran: If I'm challenging somebody, you know, what effect this is going to have on that person or their relationship with the others. But I

wouldn't verbalise it, but I acknowledge it to myself that this is going to be risky.

I: What about in terms of clients? Do you think they are taking a risk by coming into therapy?

Fran: Oh, yes … they definitely are, yes, definitely they are.

I: Do you acknowledge that to the client?

Fran: No, I just try in any way I can to make them feel safe and trusting, and (pause) I suppose that they feel secure enough, you know, to be able to take the risk.

Overall the responses to this topic did not indicate any difference between therapists' views associated with their attachment styles. However, Fran seemed to indicate preoccupation with her own safety rather than that of her clients. This may be justified to the extent that, as a private practitioner working at home, the risk was probably higher for Fran, in terms of her own emotional and physical safety. She did not have an organisation or colleagues that could support her if anything went wrong.

Other participating therapists focused more on the risks that clients encountered in discussing their issues. A few of the therapists described how taking risks and discussing private matters could only be feasible when a safe space is created for each individual member. Therapists in this study needed to use their own judgement to consider if safety could be jeopardised when family members meet together to discuss and raise their concerns.

Therapists' contribution to a shared sense of purpose within the family

Participating therapists described their contribution to a shared sense of purpose within the family, illustrating their roles in helping to improve family relations, achieve common family goals, and foster a sense of unity among the family members. Three major aspects were highlighted by most therapists: 1) they encouraged clients to compromise with each other; 2) they encouraged families to ask each other for their perspectives; and c) sometimes, they failed to address each family member's stated concerns.

There were differences in the ways the therapists encouraged clients to ask each other for their perspectives. They showed that when the task was more 'challenging' or, potentially, could create more 'conflict', therapists with secure attachment styles were better able to encourage clients than therapists with insecure attachment styles. Let us take a look at their excerpts.

Therapists encouraged clients to ask each other for their perspectives

Contributing to a family's shared sense of purpose includes encouraging family members to find out how everyone views the problems, as well as the possible solutions. Secure therapists were able to handle disagreement among family members better or were more responsive, as shown by previous research that secure therapists were able to attend to clients' underlying needs (Dozier et al., 1994).

Joan described that her job was to help clients in their relationships. For her to be able to hear the shift that clients made suggests encouraging them to change their stance or make a 'shift' from the current position to a different one that enables the other party to hear a different aspect of the problem. I can sense that her ability to facilitate the changes was important to reaffirm her self-confidence as a therapist:

> 'aaa ... (9 secs) I would say, when I saw the daughter and the father together and we talked about why she's angry, she feels let down by the father. For us to be able to talk about that, and, maybe, for the father to realise that, that was a really good thing for him and his daughter, and, at the end of the day, what my job is to mm help their relationship, not be critical, or be judgemental and for me to hear the shift mm. The daughter has been able to be honest with her father and let him know why she's feeling the way that she is. And mm ... (10 secs) maybe him feeling he's got a better understanding of why she's angry and why she's doing what she's doing, and that, in some way, I was facilitating that and I helped that to happen.'
>
> (Joan)

The notion of expressing differences and different points of views was further elaborated by Betty, who emphasised that family therapy only works if family members dare to express differences. She illustrated how, with one of the families that she saw, the mother was voicing her disagreement with the father and how she thought her son might be angry with her for doing that:

> 'I suppose the key thing I emphasised from day one is the only way family therapy works is for people to express differences, different points of view, different takes. So, I'm thinking of a family I saw the other day where the boy has serious mmm well whole range of difficulties but one of them is autistic spectrum and he's very controlling and we were doing the first session with them all and his mother expressed differences to the father, sort of saying, "well I don't see it quite like that, my thinking is" and the boy was absolutely furious with her for disagreeing. And she said "he will be cross with me now".'
>
> (Betty)

Betty then illustrated how she encouraged clients to take a step in discussing their differences in terms of views, feelings, and stories. Betty's ability to use humour and to invite clients to discuss their differences playfully was helpful in fostering a shared sense of purpose within the family. The family was able to talk about their differences, which were somewhat off limit initially. Unlike Izzy, who wanted to feel reassured by the client's changes and her role in helping to make those changes possible, I did not see this as important to Betty. Betty's confidence in her work seemed to shine through without having to state verbally her role in managing the situation:

> 'And I just said that their mother had done exactly what we would like because, actually, if this is going to be helpful, I need people to say things a little bit different. And then one of the younger ones said, "well I think differently too". And we started having them joke about who can think the most differently, the boy then joined in and said, "well, I'm different to everybody". So, just by being a bit playful, emphasizing differences are really useful. I would say that's probably a key strategy talking about different takes and I'll talk about difference, both in terms of views, but also in terms of feelings, and, also in terms of stories.'
>
> (Betty)

Additionally, Lin described talking about different stories involving being able to see from another person's perspective in order to understand that the construct that clients have built in the past might not necessarily hold true now. Therefore, hearing other's perspectives allows clients to understand each other, which, in her terms, created an *'aha moment',* signifying insights into the problem at hand. Nonetheless, Lin did not state how she encouraged clients to ask for each other's perspective. In other words, she did not describe her role as a therapist, unlike Betty, who described how she approached the situation – by using humour and being playful:

> 'And I also don't think. Some of them can, sort of, really switch ... that somebody understands differently and that's usually because let's say they've been very resentful of a past event and they can see from another person's perspective and understand it wasn't necessarily the whole construct that they built, how they behaved and why it happened and why it wasn't quite right and see the other person's point of view and that could be like an aha moment, wow, yes and suddenly it clicks. Sometimes, there's a couple who make a lovely gesture towards the other, not here necessarily but at home and suddenly she thinks, actually he does love me. I think it's not just one turning point, I think it's several. I don't know what to call them several landmarks, insight, that's the one.'
>
> (Lin)

However, Lin did conclude that asking clients questions about the other party's struggles or perspectives helps them to see each other more, which suggests that by encouraging clients to open up and listen to each other's perspectives allows them to see one another more as a whole and not merely looking from the previous schema or point of view.

Key Points 5.8

All the therapists tended to explore the clients' disagreement and differences in order to encourage family members to look at each other's perspectives. This was done by

- asking clients to talk about differences in their views, feelings, or stories; and

- asking questions that made them think of other people's struggles and perspectives.

However, the therapists differed in their confidence in handling such situations, which was associated with their attachment styles. The secure therapist (Betty) seemed to manage the situation well, using positive skills, such as humour and play, while the insecure therapists (Lin and Joan) did not describe how they encouraged clients to ask for each other's perspectives or their roles in facilitating the situation.

In fostering a shared sense of purpose within the family, there were differences in views according to therapists' attachment styles in just one of the categories discussed – therapists encouraged clients to ask each other for their perspectives – while other categories – therapists encouraged clients to compromise with each other and therapists failed to address the concerns of each family member – did not show that there were differences in their views according to their attachment styles. Thus, other factors were more relevant in fostering a shared sense of purpose within the family, such as their experience, and their ability to look at the 'common' factor of clients' experiences, as well as pointing those out to help clients find a way to problem solve their issues or find a solution.

Diversity of therapists' views on alliance building and practice

Participating therapists, regardless of attachment styles, discussed building a therapeutic alliance. Their discussions centred on the four themes in alliance building identified by Friedlander and her colleagues (Friedlander et al., 2005; Friedlander et al., 2006). There were no major differences in their views on three of the alliance dimensions: engaging in the therapeutic process, safety within the therapeutic system, and shared sense of purpose within the family. However, differences existed in the degree or depth of explanations provided by therapists with secure and insecure attachment styles. The findings show that therapists with secure attachment styles provide a softer approach, utilising humour and reasoning, while their insecure counterparts are either too strong in their approach or focus only on safety, despite acknowledging the conflict. Perhaps it is no surprise that the secure therapists were able to provide in-depth feedback, as shown in the present study. Black et al. (2005), in their study of individual psychotherapists of different orientations, found that there was a positive correlation between therapists' attachment styles and alliance; therapists with secure attachment styles showed better alliances with their clients. They also found that therapists with insecure attachment styles reported having more problems in therapy.

The therapists differed in the way they described emotional connection within the therapeutic system. The secure therapists in this study explored their personal reactions towards clients or their situations, unlike those with insecure attachment styles. Therapists with preoccupied and fearful attachment styles described their reactions but did not elaborate on how they would use such reactions in exploring clients' situations. Those with dismissing styles did not state that they would acknowledge their personal reactions. This very much relates to the idea of making sense of their experiences, the concept of 'mentalization' (Fonagy and Target, 1997) and moving from a 'rigid embedded stance to the flexibility of a mentalizing and reflecting one' (Wallin, 2007, p. 139). Wallin described how most people, without being aware, are simply embedded in their own problematic experience and not able to create an alternative view. Thus, mentalization is the awareness to create multiple perspectives when faced with any experience. By mentalizing, we are able to identify and regulate our affects in order to help us evaluate our experience and guide our subsequent action accordingly.

The ability to have such awareness very much relates to being secure and the ability to take a step further in recognizing our own issues and being able to use them in a constructive way. This was shown in the excerpts of the secure therapists where they revealed their inner experience and utilised their reactions, which acted as an insight in exploring clients' situations. Furthermore, the 'family's emotional state is likely to arouse [an] affect in the therapist' where the therapist feels she has to act and the risk of being drawn into the family's script. Therefore, being able to take a reflective stance enables therapists to understand what is happening in the family (Byng-Hall, 2008, p. 139). At the same time, Byng-Hall (2008) stated that therapists need to 'be aware of their own family scripts and the sort of scenarios that are likely to trigger their action or to draw them into adopting a particular attitude to what is going on [in] the family' (p. 140).

The therapists' stories can be related to the Attachment Narrative Therapy Model (ANT) described by Dallos and Vetere (2009) in focusing on important stories that we develop about our connections (emotional, sexually intimate relationships, attachment with others, dependencies, experiences, and expectations of trust in our relationships), where our childhood experiences form the material of our developing narratives about ourselves and others. These narratives are then transferred to other situations and relationships outside our family. The ANT model also depicts that narratives are dynamic, similar to the therapeutic process; changing through constant construction, reconstruction, and review and evoking strong feelings.

Thus, we choose where to tell our stories, who to tell, what to include and exclude, and what we want others to know. Hence, a secure base is important for us to be able to open up in discussing our issues; to challenge our current views by exploring within a systemic framework and looking at every system involved, such as our patterns of relating and attachment, and to reflect upon them. Perhaps the ability to consider an alternative story, reflect on feelings, and provide a corrective measure concerning ways we deal with our challenges shows how the secure therapists in this study challenged their own problem-saturated stories; by reconstructing new narratives that enabled them to look at their problem with a bird's eye view, from a third person's perspective. The ability to reflect and to utilise one's own experiences and realise when such experience activated their insecurity, as described by Carl regarding his complaining mother, and Betty about the death of her mother, enables these therapists to work in this emotionally demanding job in a more objective way.

Exercise 5.2 Tools for Alliance Building

- What tools can be utilised to assist therapists in their work?
- How would the tools help therapists?

Chapter summary

- This chapter described how a secure therapist is able to use his or her good or bad experience in therapy. One with a secure attachment style is able to create a secure base for his or her client and manage clients' hostility in a better way.
- The excerpts of secure therapists revealed their inner experiences and showed their reactions, which acted as insights in exploring clients' situations.
- Differences exist in the depth of explanations provided by therapists with secure and insecure attachment styles. Therapists with secure attachment styles provide a softer approach, utilising humour and reasoning, while therapists with insecure attachment styles are either too strong in their approach or focus only on safety, despite acknowledging the conflict.

6

Continuing Professional Development and the Role of Supervision

This chapter focuses on

- why therapists need continuing professional development;
- the importance of supervision;
- what therapists say about supervision; and
- the importance of training and supervision.

Why do we need continuous training as therapists?

In Chapter 3 on why therapists and counsellors need to know about attachment, we discussed the idea that attachment styles can be disrupted along our life span due to unforeseen circumstances or experiences. Nevertheless, the disruption caused by attachment activation can be repaired as the plasticity of our brain allows us to retrain our brain into thinking differently through training, therapy, and supervision, which provide new narratives to old stories or wounds. This notion that attachment style is repairable brings hope for therapists and clients alike to continuously work on the self. In writing this book, I ponder on the ingredients that we need for us to repair our attachment styles.

Exercise 6.1 What Do You Need?

- Think of your own career development, whether as a novice or experienced therapist. What has helped you in your professional career?
- List two training experiences that you found helpful. In what ways were they helpful?
- What other things do you want to happen in your professional life? How might you achieve this?

There are many possible answers to the questions on career development. For example, some therapists highlight having a great supervisor as the most important help in their professional career. Additionally, some research (Lambert and Lawson, 2013; Norcross, 2000) suggests that self-care is an essential component. Further training sessions (Nel, 2006; Williams et al., 2015) can be helpful in developing an understanding of the self of the therapist, such as training on knowing one's attachment style and what might activate our attachment insecurity. Additionally, personal therapy or confiding in a trusted individual, such as a family member or a good friend, has been reported to be beneficial to many therapists, especially when setbacks occur that can potentially help in the therapist's growth and development, as described by Brown (2012) on vulnerability.

Brown (2012), in her book *Daring Greatly,* defined vulnerability as 'uncertainty, risk, and emotional exposure' (p. 34). She discussed how the courage to be vulnerable is the key to wholehearted living. However, vulnerability without boundaries leads to disconnection. Brown (2012) further explained that pushing vulnerability away disables our ability to expose ourselves to uncertainty, risk, and the emotional exposure of joy. Vulnerability (shown by 'secure' therapists in my study as they are more open to discussing their struggles) is essential if the professional desires to work on improving themselves as therapists. Vulnerability allows people to reflect and appreciate the beauty and imperfections in one's life, which very much reflect on metacognitive functioning in the attachment sense, where we build new working models and give new narratives to old stories. Hence, vulnerability allows us to acknowledge our soft spots to the right people – people that we have formed good relationships with – which will lead to increase connection, trust, and engagement. One might then ask, how do we achieve this? Although we cannot control our upbringing or unforeseen things that happened in our lives, such as death or loss, we can exercise control over how we view these situations.

So, what do therapists or counsellors need in order to cultivate vulnerability? This is when the role of supervisors comes into play. A supervisor is similar to the aspects of the therapist's role to clients that can parallel the caregiver's roles, where a supervisor constructively challenges the supervisee's misguided ideas or interpretation and points out the strengths and weaknesses of a decision. The supervisor has the capacity to give third-person perspectives, providing feedback and support when and as needed by the supervisee. Being open and truthful in supervision is essential; as Brown (2012) stated, by practicing courage, compassion, and connection in our daily lives, we are able to cultivate worthiness. Being vulnerable is an act of courage. A therapist who opens up to his or her supervisor about the daily struggles he or she is facing in sessions or things that are hindering therapeutic relationships is being courageous and is acting compassionately towards himself or herself before being compassionate to clients. This, in turn, will lead to better connection, specifically better therapeutic alliances.

Exercise 6.2 Cultivating Vulnerability

- Think of your own strengths and weaknesses.
- List your strengths that might help you in building good relationships.
- List your weaknesses that might hinder your relationships with clients.
- Do you think your attachment style plays a role in your relationship with clients, supervisors, and other people? How?
- Would you discuss this with a supervisor? Why or why not?

There are strengths that can lead to building good therapeutic relationships. In a helping profession, it is a standard recommendation for therapists to have excellent communication, interview, and observation skills. Weaknesses that might hinder therapeutic alliance include unresolved issues on the part of the therapists and not realising when referrals should be made if therapists are stuck in unproductive countertransference. The interviews with therapists in my study showed that attachment style plays a major role in relationship building, especially when attachment insecurity is activated. My own research shows the benefits of discussing issues with supervisors, preferably those from a different agency, as revealed by one of the therapists in the interviews (Yusof and Carpenter, 2016). Personally, I think having someone outside the agency might be beneficial for therapists. How then might a supervisor or a training centre play a role?

The importance of training and supervision

It is probably disheartening if we discover that our attachment styles are 'insecure'. We might even question if we are even cut out to be therapists. We now know that attachment styles, despite their stability in childhood, can be disrupted due to major life events, such as the death of a family member, a terminal illness, or a separation and vice versa. This means that security might be disrupted, but an adult with a secure attachment style may be able to find support and not be paralysed by the situation, for example, avoiding or dismissing the conflict at hand. So, a therapist with an insecure attachment style needs to work on himself or herself in order to be 'healthily available' to clients. Thus, when disruption occurs and when attachment insecurities are activated, these might not be all bad for therapists. Therapists who learn from such experiences are often able to reframe their issues and become more successful at noticing when their attachment insecurities are activated.

In the interviews, it was revealed that there were other factors that therapists viewed as important in building good alliances with clients, including having a supportive environment, which includes good supervision and working in a team. However, before we look at what therapists said about supervision, let us review the literature.

The exploration of the 'self' of the therapist, as part of the skill acquisition in becoming a therapist, should be part of our continuous professional development. Alves de Oliveira and Vandenberghe (2009), in their study of upsetting experiences faced by therapists, suggested that in-session stressors constitute only one aspect of therapists' distress. The therapist as a person and his or her vulnerabilities, coping styles, and skills in using self are important variables when facing upsetting events in real-life clinical practice.

Jennings et al. (2003) described various factors that contribute to the expertise of therapists. Beyond spending more time in practice and gaining experience, other factors include emotional and relational characteristics, openness to change, cultural competence, and comfort with ambiguity. Thus, according to them, a successful practitioner's development includes continuously striving towards mastery and having awareness in the ambiguity of the work. This ambiguity points to the importance of training and supervision, about which I postulated that therapists who are aware of their selves and challenges would then be able to look at them objectively. Such awareness can be achieved, and one way to achieve this is through supervision and training. Therapy is a two-way process and therapists co-create meanings with their clients. Reducing threats in therapy is part of a process in creating rapport with clients. In order to create a non-threatening environment, therapists need to 1) be aware of how they are being perceived and 2) strive to remove the elements that cause threats (Combs, 1989), including their own issues or belief system. Reflexivity, as shown by secure therapists, can help therapists to respond according to the specific needs that best fit the client at that particular time and in that particular context (Hedges, 2010). It could be seen that this was displayed by therapists with secure attachment styles, where they were able to utilise their experiences in their practice and respond sensitively to their clients.

We now know that supervisors may create a safe space in supervision similar to the role of therapists in providing safety to clients. In therapy, the supervisor must create an atmosphere of trust for the supervisee to be open and honest about what takes place in therapy. According to Rosenbaum and Ronen (1998), the question of trust, however, may be more problematic in the supervisory relationship, because it is understandable that in therapy, the client's needs supersede the therapist's needs. In supervision, 'therapists and supervisors may not share the same theoretical orientation, leading to apprehension or scepticism, and the supervisee may not be committed to complete honesty and openness' (Rosenbaum and Ronen, 1998, p. 225). Mistrust could also be the product of the multiple roles carried by supervisors. Supervisors who have an institutional responsibility over the therapist's work are also responsible to the institution, its clients, and the treatment of clients by therapists (Rosenbaum and Ronen, 1998).

Hence, therapists might not be able to be secure enough to bring what transpired in therapy to supervisors if they feel threatened by the supervisor's institutional role, and this may defeat the purpose of supervision, which is meant to empower and provide constructive feedback to therapists. One suggestion is probably to employ supervisors from different agencies, as stated by one of the therapists in my study (Izzy). One might also think of whether attachment helps or hinders supervisory relationships. Nevertheless, clinical supervision differs from management supervision. An external clinical supervisor may be more acceptable to some practitioners for the purpose of discussing situations involving the impact of their personal issues on their practice. However, in issues pertaining to the self and how they impact on practice, the external supervisor might be more suitable since it might be awkward (as described by therapists), for therapists to disclose issues to someone from one's own agency, probably fearing that this might impact future performance or the other's perception or might escalate to the point that confidentiality and professionalism are compromised.

Nevertheless, in public service organisations, such as social and health services, the practitioner's line manager is always responsible for supervising the management of cases. An external clinical supervisor is not accountable to the agency and must not assume case responsibility, implicitly or explicitly. Issues such as a breach of data protection, safeguarding a child or vulnerable adult, or a deliberate self-harm must be reported to the line manager without delay. The personal impact on the practitioner may subsequently be examined with an external clinical supervisor, but this must never be a replacement for discussion and decision-making with the line manager.

Based on previous chapters, I hope you now agree that knowing your attachment style and how and when your attachment system is activated might prove useful in managing relationships, specifically therapeutic relationships. Thus, this can be achieved through continuous professional training and supervision, as they are tools to provide awareness and to make better sense of the interplay between the self of the therapist and the therapist's experiences. Anderson and Swim (1995) suggested the idea of supervision as a collaborative process in which both the supervisor and the supervisee create narratives and stories in the supervisory process. Similar to the idea of reflexive functioning, supervision can give voice to new context or meaning, which, in turn, leads to learning and change.

We can now agree that good supervision is one the keys in the making of a successful therapist. Therapists might be exposed to vicarious trauma or compassionate fatigue and having a supervisor can help to process the day-to-day challenges in therapeutic work. The supervisor is the facilitator or mentor who navigates self-reflective learning. Supervision helps the supervisee or trainee to learn the profession, involving, among others, theory, skills, induction into a profession, professional savvy and wisdom, self-awareness, ethical awareness and sensitivity, and the ability to use intuition and knowledge, attitudes, values, and mindsets that help to build the professional regardless of his or her profession (Carroll, 2010). The focus should be the future. What would you do differently from your past learning?

What therapists say about supervision

All therapists should be having supervision as part of their professional development. It is probably safe to conclude that supervision is essential in good therapeutic work. We are in a way limited by our knowledge and experience. Hence, there are things that we might dismiss or overlook due to certain limitations, such as that we are simply 'stuck', or we lack certain experience that others might have insight into. The insights of other professionals are where supervision plays a supportive role.

This was exemplified by Izzy when she described her emotional pain in trying to support her clients. She elaborated on the importance of having a support network and good supervision. Nonetheless, she further claimed that her supervisor did not need to know everything about her ('I don't think she needs to know everything'). However, one gets the sense that she would let her supervisor know if she thought that she needed to inform the supervisor of an issue or to get a third person's perspective:

I: How did you deal with trying to support them while you yourself were dealing with some pain at that time?

Izzy: Well, I think, some of it is about having my own support network and mm having very good supervision which doesn't mean... of course, my supervisor knows a bit about me and my life because I have a long trusting relationship with this supervisor... She doesn't know everything and doesn't need to know everything, and, really, I don't think she needs to know everything, if she needs [to know] I would [tell her].'

After thinking for a few seconds, she went on to reiterate the important aspect of supervision. Supervision helped her to process the details of the therapeutic relationship for the therapist's own well-being and to provide a better service:

> '... (10 secs) so supervision is a very important aspect, a hugely important aspect. Supervision, I mean consultation, so it's not sort of managerial. I mean, in terms of real process, talking about the therapy, what it does for me, what it does for clients, how we work.'
>
> (Izzy)

She also stated that she was quite uneasy with the current situation, in which the NHS restructuring might mean the end of external consultation, so that supervision will be provided by colleagues within the same Trust. Izzy asserted that this would create a difference in terms of the things that will be taken into supervision, suggesting an impact on the safety of the therapist. The therapists might think that their confidentiality is not guaranteed, and, hence, may be reluctant to bring their own personal issues into supervision:

> '... that's (supervision) for me ... (3 secs) crucial, central, in fact I'm quite concerned with the way things are going. In the end, the NHS is chopping right, front, left and centre. The first thing that's going is the external

consultation, which is your confidential separate space to take your things to. So, you're now meant to do it within your own Trust, which of course ... (4 secs) makes a big difference to what you take to your supervision, I think.'

(Izzy)

The importance of supervision was further discussed by George. He explained that supervision not only helps but is an essential part of the therapeutic process:

'Supervision I think is essential; I don't think it just helps. Well it helps I think in a major way.'

(George)

Supervision also provides an insight for therapists to look at clients' issues differently. This was illustrated by Eleanor when she described having new ideas and suggestions concerning how to handle things. In her own words:

'I have very good supervision and it's always good to get new ideas and not to assume that, you know, you've tried everything. People often have very different suggestions about different ways of moving things forward.'

(Eleanor)

Additionally, Joan described being aware of her own life story and would discuss it with her supervisor. This indicates that supervision is not just about processing what is happening in therapy but also provides a sense of balance for the therapists who juggle their own issues in providing support to clients. The finding also showed that Joan was quite hesitant to answer the question. She paused for a few seconds and provided a very brief answer:

I: Going back to when you talked about bereavement in your own experience, sometimes we come to cases that are, sort of, similar to our own life stories, so does that impact on your work as a therapist and how do you deal with that?

Joan: How do I deal with it? Mm ... (12 secs) I'm aware of it and I will talk about it.

I: with the client (cut by Joan)

Joan: no ... no ... whoever I was having supervision with and I have worked with somebody who was in a very similar position.

The importance of supervision was further highlighted by Fran. Similar to Joan, she also described turning to supervision to process her emotions:

Fran: Physically mm ... well I felt emotionally unsafe in the child protection one and it turned out that I was right to do so because they made a complaint, so I felt emotionally unsafe, anxious.

I: What did you do when that happened?

Fran: Well, when I finished the session I talked to my supervisor (both laughed). But, in the session, I just sort of bear it.

On a different occasion, Fran, who is now a private practitioner, stressed the crucial role that supervision played in her development as a therapist. She also described the anxiety of working alone without the luxury of an agency full of other therapists and how this heightened her awareness of the issue:

> 'It's essential to have good supervision. I have two supervisors, peer supervision group. I find that's very essential. But, obviously, there are times when they are not available or it's not the right time or whatever. I think I do find working on my own, it can be very worrying at times. It can be worrying at times because, if you are in a clinic, you've got all your colleagues around and you can just chat to them but if you're on your own you can't talk to your other colleagues. I'm aware that it's in me and I have to be, and I noticed probably after two or three days it's gone but I've got to be aware of that.'
>
> (Fran)

The therapists' accounts revealed that supervision is an integral part of practice and of professional growth. The importance of supervision reflects the need for therapists to be supported. It is particularly significant for private practitioners, such as Fran, who are not supported by an agency or colleagues at hand. Izzy described the security of being supervised by someone outside her agency. This probably reflects the anxiety of being scrutinised by members of one's own organisation. The excerpts of interviews also demonstrated that security might play a role in the therapists' need for supervision. The therapists who described the importance of supervision were insecure therapists.

Key Points 6.1

- Supervision is helpful regardless of attachment styles.
- Therapists with secure attachment styles did not touch on the need for supervision, but this does not necessarily reflect that secure therapists viewed supervision as less important. Simply that they did not touch on this issue, unlike their counterparts with insecure attachment styles. However, whether the need for supervision relates to attachment security is unknown. Nevertheless, we are limited in terms of the knowledge that we possess; hence, we might overlook things or dismiss important things that might be helpful in assisting clients. Therefore, it is always beneficial to have supervision.

Therapists described the importance of good supervision to process what took place in therapy. The therapists' narratives were similar to other research, which also recognised the importance of supervision in therapeutic work (Savic-Jabrow, 2010; Orchowski et al., 2010). One therapist described the anxiety caused by the NHS restructuring, which meant that external consultation might no longer be available. This was seen as a limitation, suggesting that supervision should, ideally, be given by someone who is not from the same agency as the therapist. Carroll (2010) stated that supervision provides a new way of looking at things that brings new perspectives and new meanings. Indeed, supervision is an integral part of practice, and, perhaps, the idea of 'baring it all' to someone known or familiar makes the particular therapist in this study feel anxious to self-reflect. However, her concern also probably reflects her fearful attachment style.

Supervision is probably more salient to lone practitioners, as reflected by Fran in her comments. Working alone as a private practitioner exposed her to more anxiety when facing critical situations, without the support offered by being able to refer to other colleagues. Fran's concerns were shared in previous findings on support received by counsellors in private practice (Savic-Jabrow, 2010). All the participants whom I interviewed identified the supervisory process as an important aspect of their work as a private practitioner. Savic-Jabrow (*ibid.*) also described that, without access to colleagues, supervision is of greater influence to independent practitioners as it is probably the only avenue to provide an opportunity for the therapist to reflect on their work and the impact on themselves. For example, in the UK, a framework in systemic family therapy, 'Improving Access to Psychological Therapies' (IAPT), was proposed to address arising issues in delivering effective services through designing better training courses. The aim is to prepare practitioners who are confident and competent to deliver good practices. One of the important elements in IAPT is the supervisory role (Karamat Ali and Bachicha, 2012). The authors described that 'therapists needed to acknowledge the influences of their own beliefs, cognitions and assumptions, and the impact such influences had on their evaluations during their work' (p. 201). This is when the notion of the 'safe space' promoted by Bowlby (1988a) is extended beyond the therapeutic room to the realm of the supervisory room. Thus, being vulnerable, as discussed in the beginning of this chapter, and becoming self-reflexive, can only take place when the space is safe.

Key Points 6.2

Why do we need continuous training as a therapist? The problems surrounding us evolve as the world evolves. Issues that were not an issue a decade ago surface due to many factors: the fast life that we live in, rapid changes, and the use of technology. Continuous training is essential in order to keep abreast of the current practice and to be aware of the research findings that will help us in practice.

Supervision is essential, especially for lone practitioners. Supervision is best provided by an external supervisor, someone not from the same agency.

Increased reflexivity

The therapists' experiences suggested that therapists with insecure attachment styles might have challenges in therapeutic encounters with families, especially when they are challenged and their attachment styles are activated. Thus, clinical supervision might increase understanding of the self and encourage novice therapists' awareness of their own responses, which help them when they are in sessions with clients (Wittenborn, 2012). This is important not just for novice practitioners but also for experienced practitioners (Yusof and Carpenter, 2016), and can be achieved through increased self-reflexivity. Thus, a therapist's self-reflexivity concerning how their personal experiences informed their therapeutic works can be increased through supervision.

Exercise 6.3 Supervision and Self-Reflexivity

- Do you agree that supervision provides a safe space that helps to increase self-reflexivity in practice?
- Reflect on your own practice. List two conditions that you think might facilitate reflexivity.

One condition that can facilitate reflexivity relates to therapists' experiential work with their own families. For example, McCandless and Eatough's (2012) therapists in training emphasised the importance of exploring their understanding of their family of origin in developing self-reflexivity. This is where an understanding of therapists' attachment styles might be useful in recreating new scripts to heal an old 'wound' in response to attachment activated when facing the experienced threat. Similar to the notion of providing safety to clients, supervision needs to provide a safe space to support the learning and teaching environment. This parallels the idea of a 'secure base', which allows supervisees to take risks. McCandless and Eatough (2012) showed that an unsafe environment will create barriers for the supervisee. In other words, supervisees will put up a front to mask their true feelings and will not discuss the threats they encounter in therapy. This results in preventing vulnerability or risk taking in learning from taking place. How then do we encourage therapists' self-reflexivity?

Exercise 6.4 Self-Reflexivity and Family of Origin

- Think of your own family of origin. What aspect in your family of origin increases your understanding in your work as a therapist?
- Did your personal experience influence your therapeutic work? How?

How did you feel when doing exercise 6.4? It is probably difficult for some therapists to describe their feelings in completing this exercise. In drafting this exercise, I drew on Mason's (2012) insight that the story of our core beliefs and the development thereof influences our personal and professional lives. When I think of my own development, I draw on how Islam shapes the way I lead my life. It is probably difficult to separate one's personal beliefs and professional life. For example, being a practising Muslim influences my everyday decisions because everything I do revolves around religious practices.

Regardless of religious belief or having no such beliefs, a broad 'ethical' umbrella governs our conduct towards our fellow human beings. Thus, it is important to always check our assumptions and biases, and this is when supervision is important. Mason (2002) re-emphasised Hoffman's (1985) point about the act of the observer-dependent perspective as a crucial development for family of origin issues in training. According to the author, therapists are not independent from the clients they observe. Therapists' own contexts are an integral part of therapeutic relationships. They can no longer sit outside without influencing or being influenced by the therapeutic process. This highlights the need for therapists to consider the systemic nature of therapeutic relationships and questions how they are influencing or being influenced by their clients. As Hoffman (1985) explained, therapists can no longer be detached observers; they are part of the world they observe, which promotes the process of reflexive practice. An experienced practitioner might be comfortable to act on his or her intuitive clinical knowledge.

Nevertheless, there will be times when the therapist is unable to articulate his or her know-how, which invites therapists to trust in his or her intuition and tacit knowledge (Cutcliffe, 2003). Being confident of one's knowledge and decisions is a learning process that can be done with the help of a supervisor or a colleague, as this might spark more questions of oneself when therapists or practitioners engage in the process of self-reflexivity. To avoid blind spots that might lead to wrong decision-making, I suggest that therapists be attentive in keeping a record of their thoughts and therapeutic acts. This is because there is a tendency for 'inappropriate and overzealous self-criticism' when a therapist is unable to explain his or her insight regarding a reflexive account (Cutcliffe, 2003, p. 146).

For more than 20 years, the criteria for accreditation for training courses in family therapy and family therapy supervision in the UK has addressed family of origin issues (Mason et al., 2002). Despite this, many of the therapists in my study revealed struggles concerning these (Yusof and Carpenter, 2014), which suggests the need for an ongoing personal and professional development programme. Good training enables the enhancement of reflexive awareness in supervisees, where changes occur in both the supervisee's inner processes and their outer responses (McCandless and Eatough, 2012). Therefore, the role of the supervisor is to provide a safe space, to encourage reflexive accountability, challenge compassionately, and provide constructive feedback in order for trust to develop in the supervisory relationship. Mason further argued that the 'ability to take risks and stay with tension within oneself, with clients and within the therapeutic system' is part of the process of becoming a good therapist. Thus, he suggested that therapists should explore difficult issues and themes in their own lives. This involves taking risks in exploring their relationships through time, across relationships, and across contexts and examining the meanings for therapists to risk culturally (p. 47).

Despite the weight of exploring such issues, these reflections can assist therapists in training or post-training to develop a more effective practice when they are able to observe internally and be aware of how their family of origin issues and culture play a role in developing the self. Mason et al. (2002) provided some examples for self-reflexivity, such as the role or impact that family of origin or culture has on the self when being criticised, being challenged, and handling adversity. Nevertheless, it is important to acknowledge that such an exercise, while essential, can be dangerous without support and structure. In order to conduct such an emotional process, 'the therapists have to be clear about his or her own emotional process, and have had the experience of being held in a therapeutic process themselves, so that they have an emotional map of what's going on (Mason et al., 2002, p. 48). Hence, supervision and consultation are important, as Mason et al. stated that the 'family of origin training is symbolic of our inclusiveness and accountability.

To separate the personal from the political, the emotional from the technical, may well have "diabolical" consequences!' (p. 49). Having discussed the importance and the challenges of family of origin issues, try to complete exercise 6.5 and reflect on your own family of origin.

Exercise 6.5 Genogram and Family of Origin

- Draw a genogram of your own family of origin.
- Reflect on the process of drawing and the genogram itself. Is there any memory that is warm, makes you smile, or evokes strong feelings? Why?
- Would you discuss this with a colleague or a supervisor? List at least two reasons as to why you would or would not.

Besides family of origin, Totsuka (2014) explained that understanding issues of diversity related to gender, geography, race, religion, age, ability, appearance, class, culture, ethnicity, education, sexuality, sexual orientation, and spirituality (Burnham, 2012) can increase a supervisee's reflexivity, and that this could be achieved through training and supervision. Exercise 6.6 aims to increase your awareness regarding the roles that the differences listed by Burnham play in your therapeutic relationship.

Exercise 6.6 Self-Reflexivity and Diversity

This exercise is based on Totsuka (2014) in respect of differences and self-reflexivity:

- Think of your own background. Based on gender, geography, race, religion, age, ability, appearance, class, culture, ethnicity, education, sexuality, sexual orientation, and spirituality (Burnham, 2012), choose whether any of these differences relate to you.
- Describe whether what you chose makes you feel privileged or discriminated. Why?
- How do you think the differences you listed play a role in building or hindering your relationship with your client?

The exercise above aims to address therapists' own assumptions and biases, which are sometimes overlooked due to our unconscious biases. Mason (2012) suggested that therapists should be more transparent about their own life stories and core beliefs and where they are situated in the therapeutic relationship. Transparency about our core beliefs can potentially help us navigate our professional tasks. For example, a therapist needs to find a position within the therapeutic relationship in which differences are not exacerbated to the point that the only thing that we see in each other is our differences. This reflects upon our daily experiences of meeting people different from us where the way we act, speak, or the language we choose play important roles in bridging the gap between cultures. The self could be viewed as the direct expression of self and the indirect utilisation of self (Mason et al., 2002). The indirect utilisation of self stems from our relationship with our experiences, where issues from our families of origin are indirectly utilised. On the other hand, in the direct expression of self, therapists are encouraged to speak openly about the aspects of their histories that impact on the therapeutic alliance. The ability to utilise the self directly or indirectly relates to the idea of the secure base in the attachment theory.

Coming full circle

My interviews with the therapists provided a huge learning experience for me, and, I hope, for the therapists themselves.

It brings me full circle in terms of my experience researching adult attachment-related issues and writing this book. As described in the introduction, many years ago in my training in the United States, I questioned whether therapists play a role in the therapeutic relationship and I attributed the 'failure' of a therapeutic relationship to various factors, one of them being the differences between myself and the families I encountered. You can imagine how upsetting the experience was, not understanding that there might be other hidden factors that I as a novice contributed to the therapeutic alliance. Little did I know back then that the self of the therapists, and the taxing nature of caring for others, require a lot of self-care on the part of the therapist.

In coming full circle, I reflected on my own journey when I first started my interpersonal training in the United States and the challenges that I went through as a beginning therapist, which later coincided with the events of September 11, 2001. As a Muslim novice female practitioner, I struggled to compose myself during this difficult time and questioned my objectivity as a therapist, and how I could best help clients when I myself was a total wreck after 9/11. In the wake of the challenges immediately after 9/11, I felt quite unsupported. However, I understood that my colleagues and supervisors were as shocked as I was and were probably unable to be emotionally available to me because they themselves were going through one of the most trying times in their lives as Americans. One would think as therapists and therapists in training in the mental health centre, we were equipped with the necessary training and skills to face such challenges. Nonetheless, nothing ever prepares one to face such a catastrophe, especially for someone who works cross-culturally. As a Muslim, post 9/11, I cringed every time I heard mention of my religion being associated with terror.

The centre closed for a day for stress debriefing and opened for business as usual the very next day. I met my first client on 12 September 2001, a nine-year-old girl. In the wake of 9/11, it felt ironic how the therapeutic relationship was helpful for Jane (pseudonym), as well as for myself as her therapist. To this day, I recall the conversation that I had with Jane, one day after the horrific incident. That was the first time that Jane ever asked me about my nationality, and I showed her the globe to explain my origin. This little child then told me about her Arab friends and that not everyone is bad, which attests to her wonderful upbringing. As the session ended, we walked through the centre's corridor and she stopped in front of a patchwork tapestry, hanging on display, that depicted children of different colours holding hands, standing around the globe. That moment is forever pasted in my brain as Jane touched my hand, showing kindness and solidarity. Reflecting now, I understand the meaning of 'showing attachment' or communicating attachment, as described by Schore and Schore (2008). I can now say that as a trainee back then, and a Muslim from a different culture, I developed attachment to the impact of my positive encounter with Jane when facing difficult clients or situations. Like a zombie, I survived that day and the day after and put all my focus on helping the service users, not recognising the impact that the experience had on me. Fast forward to the present day; now I notice my distress when crossing borders, which has never been easy since 9/11. Every time I face immigration challenges, I remind myself that the airport security and immigration personnel are just doing their jobs.

Frawley O'Dea (2003) elaborated upon her experience as a therapist post 9/11 and suggested that each therapist will form their own relationship with 9/11 and everything following. Therapists may work through the issue, split it off, refine it, and continuously do more work for recovery. The experience can parallel other traumatic experiences in life. However, a therapist, like other public service workers, such as first responders, the police, and social workers, may encounter greater challenges than most people when facing a catastrophic event, as they still have to show up at work and be present for their clients. Thus, continued training on the impact of personal experience on the professional self is important. Therefore, I suggest that the introduction of reflexive cross-cultural and intercultural training should be considered in trying to understand our baggage and what we bring with us in our work with service users.

In researching attachment and alliance, my attachment insecurity was once again activated when my marriage collapsed, and I started to question life, especially with the anxiety of becoming a sole parent of two young children. This was when I sought support spiritually, therapeutically, and through the help of my family and network. This was aggravated by the death of my father, one of my biggest supporters in life. While writing this book, my mother passed away. Different than the unexpected death of my father, my mother was unconscious and hospitalised a few days prior to her death. Although she was unconscious, the fact that I had the opportunity to care for her helped to close the gap between life and death. Compared to my father's sudden death, my mother's death provided a different perspective. The grieving was processed differently as I was able to hold her hands and bid farewell. Perhaps, the importance of attachment lies in the memories we built with our loved ones because despite death and separation, the memories stay and will be transmitted from generation to generation. My decision to write this book initially was purely to impart knowledge. I found that therapists' narratives are poignant and their experience mirroring other colleagues who hopefully can identify and work on the self in achieving a better practice. In narrating it, I found new narratives and solace in the ways that I looked at the interviewees and their 'wounds' and mine. This is also a spiritual process for me in learning about myself, challenging old ideas, and constructing new meanings that I want to bring forward in life.

Writing this book also allows me to reflect on the many students I have had the opportunity to supervise for practicums and the ways in which their own issues either helped or hindered their fieldwork. The opportunity to do research in this area and to look at whether attachment plays a role in therapeutic alliance further increased my understanding of the importance of the self of the practitioners in the work that we do. For example, for social workers, potential stressors come from the demand of their 'high caseloads, high acuity, and client turnover' (Pack, 2013, p. 3). These factors, coupled with the daily challenges of the medical model of assessment and treatment, produce a host of potential stressors in the workplace. These stressors extend beyond the social workers' clients and their traumatisation, to their interactions with the system in which they work (Pack, 2013). Perhaps this is best described by Norcross (2000), who elaborated that practitioners study and modify other humans. Thus, 'psychological principles, methods, and research are rarely brought to bear on therapists themselves' (p. 710), except in an attempt to diagnose one another. It is probably not unique that in caring for others, practitioners or therapists often neglect their own self-care. How then do we help each other?

Through researching attachment styles, and how they relate to the therapeutic alliance, I learnt that each of the therapists I interviewed, whatever their adult attachment style and experiences in their family of origin, aspired to be the best therapist they can be. I also realised that I too contributed to the therapists' narratives, to the extent they invoked feelings within me. Trained in interpersonal practice, I had embarked on my research journey feeling confident that I would be able to understand and empathise with the therapists' work. I started with the idea of similarity between my education and those of the therapists. However, during the journey, I realised the complexities of being an outsider in trying to understand therapists who come from various backgrounds. My identity was intriguing to some participants, and I was made aware of the differences when they indicated their curiosity about me through verbal and non-verbal reactions. At times, I felt uneasy by the questions some of them raised and by the emotions evoked by some of the interviewees. Conversely, it was easy to identify with others who were warm and friendly and who told stories that were somewhat similar to my own.

My research revealed how adult attachment styles play a role in how we connect with others in therapy. The depth of reflection and the ability to be reflexive characterised therapists with secure attachment styles. They were able to use their experiences, regardless of whether they were positive or challenging, to inform their therapeutic work, whereas their counterparts with insecure attachment styles struggled to do so when therapy became difficult. The therapists' accounts revealed that our past experiences and our family of origin impact on the way we build our therapeutic relationship. Thus, in this demanding job, it is important for practitioners to forge new meanings when their past or present experiences cloud their judgements, especially in the event of countertransference. Hence, self-care entails the ability to seek continuous professional support in optimising their roles as practitioners. As I have explained, this can be achieved through formal training and clinical supervision.

Self-care

The brain's plasticity is constantly changing due to social and environmental forces. 'The circuitry implicated in social and emotional behaviour is among those circuits that appear importantly shaped by experience, and early experience in these domains likely plays a key role in governing differences among individuals in their vulnerability or resilience to future adversity' (Davidson and McEwan, 2012, p. 1). The plasticity of our brain means that we are open to the danger of absorbing the negative experience of others. This is probably salient for therapists who are constantly bombarded with clients' issues and might face vicarious trauma. Furthermore, Levine (2007) explained that therapists put on a persona, which encompasses all the presentations of self that are displayed to the clients whether intended or unintended, conscious or unconscious, tacit or explicit, and episodic or continuous acts and utterances (p. 88). Levine (2007) argued that mistakes can occur despite knowing who we are or having the ability to predict our own future responses. She further reinforced that it would be 'problematic to consider the self a knowable, enduring, and stable entity' (p. 89). Therapists might face challenges that prove too much for them to handle. In her survey on therapists' personal problems and treatment, Deutsch (1985) reported that many therapists in her study experienced relationship, depression, and other personal problems. Hence, self-care and the ability for therapists to manage their personal and professional lives are essential skills that must be cultivated. Perhaps it is difficult not to acknowledge the impact that our professional lives can have on the personals or vice-versa. How then do we practice self-care?

Exercise 6.7 Your Own Self-Care Activities

Think of your own practice and life as a practitioner. List a few things that you have incorporated as part of your self-care routines. Describe why these routines have worked for you.

Once you have completed exercise 6.7, look at some of the strategies suggested by Norcross (2000) below. Some suggestions that might be useful in your practice include:

- Openly recognising the potential side effects of interpersonal practice. You may find yourself over-personalising their sources of stress even though they are part of doing therapeutic work. Thus, it is in itself therapeutic to be able to depersonalise negative feelings associated with therapeutic work and realise that the inevitable stress of therapeutic work and what therapists are going through are universal to many therapists. Accepting this fact is the first step in taking corrective actions.
- Utilising strategies embedded within multiple therapeutic orientations. Historically, effective strategies are associated with behavioural, experiential, psychodynamic, and systemic traditions. My study showed that therapists would not adhere to only one therapeutic orientation when approaching clients' issues. This is a good thing as there is a similarity among therapists regardless of their theoretical orientation, which suggests that they are pragmatic and eclectic, when facing challenges. For example, the therapists I interviewed were also inclined towards eclectic practice or using what works in working with clients. Analysing an issue from multiple perspectives increases the probability of finding the right solution. Thus, this can be extended to their own self-care, as Norcross (2000) suggested that they need to utilise multiple strategies across orientations. Hence, it is advisable for therapists

not to stick with one particular strategy or model but to have a variety of skills to help self-change. In caring for themselves, therapists need to emphasise developing helping relationships, as Norcross (2000) contended that 'psychotherapists find helping relationships to be both satisfying and efficacious for themselves' (p. 712). Helping relationships can vary from being personal, such as in loving relationships or friendships, to professional help, such as in supervision or peer support groups. The importance of having such support was also mentioned by the therapists I interviewed, particularly for lone therapists who did not have the luxury of organisational support.

- Diversifying of professional activities. Norcross (2000) also suggested that therapists diversify their professional activities. This is probably essential in the long run to avoid burnout. Diversifying your professional activities includes diversifying your therapeutic methods (couple and family, group work, individual work), activities (psychotherapy, assessment, supervision, teaching, research), types of clients, and problems (cross-cultural, age, diagnosis, issues). Additionally, diversifying therapeutic methods, activities, or clients whom therapists meet allows an array of new experiences to enter one's life, which spark the feelings of 'newness' towards the self and the therapeutic work.

It is important to note that different self-care strategies are relevant for different people (Norcross and Guy, 2007). They acknowledged that their work as therapists is 'enriched, nourished, and privileged' (p. 18), but the work changes the individuals. Hence, self-care is an ethical obligation required for practitioners to compassionately care for their clients or otherwise risk burn-out. Other authors have listed many self-care strategies, as discussed below.

Religion and spirituality

My training in the West did not touch on the element of the therapists' religion or spirituality as a support or as a way to ground an individual when facing challenges. My personal experience when facing challenges, however, showed me how I mobilised my religion as a coping mechanism. Other authors (Vandenberghe et al., 2012; Aponte, 1998) have also shown the impact of religious and spiritual practices in promoting coping and resilience. For example, Vandenberghe et al. (2012) interviewed Brazilian therapists about their views on spirituality and religion in psychotherapy. The therapists narrated that spirituality and religion are professional assets that helped alliances, even with clients of different religious backgrounds. The authors described that the features of spirituality and religion are not combined in one concept. Self-transcendence helps to overcome therapists' distortions regarding their preferences and set ideas that impose on client issues. This helps therapists to cope with 'personally threatening themes' that might activate their attachment insecurities, while assisting them in 'taking a productive stance toward thorny client issues' (p. 10). Aponte (1998) used spirituality in a broader sense that refers to the meaning, purpose, and values in people's lives. He illustrated how his moral roots as a Puerto Rican with a Catholic background play a role in his work as a therapist. As professionals, Aponte advocated that therapists should 'learn to think and talk clearly about the spiritual platform, and work with it responsibly' (p. 38).

Social networks and support

Social networks or support groups are an important factor in caring for oneself. Harrison and Westwood (2009) described how the therapists in their study reported the importance of personal networks, such as families and friends, and how these help the therapists to maintain balance between their professional and personal lives. Social networks provide support when in need or, to use an attachment term, provide solace or a safe space to return to when distraught. The therapists found joy in their relationships to counterbalance the repeated suffering stories they encountered daily in their practices. This helped them to be centred or to maintain the equilibrium, especially when professional concerns evoke countertransference.

Physical and mental care

Physical and mental care are crucial to maintain the personal and professional selves. Williams et al. (2003) described how novice therapists tended to rely on relaxation techniques and clinical supervision to refocus their therapeutic practice, whereas their experienced colleagues relied on vacations and self-reflection outside of therapy. Readers may notice that this author used the term 'self-reflection'. According to Boud (1999), the term 'reflection' is a common term depending on the school of thought. Other common terms include reflective practice, metacognition, critical reflection and reflexivity. Despite use of similar words, the focus of each term is different. Reflection focuses on learning, reflective practice on professional practice, metacognition on knowledge, critical reflection on the political-social aspect and reflexivity on the identity. Hence, in the field of therapeutic practice or practitioner – client relationships, self-reflexivity involves an in-depth introspection of the self of the professional, which I believe include all aspects of 'reflection'. It is probably true that the experienced therapist relies less on relaxation techniques and clinical supervisions as shown by Williams et al.'s study. However, my own research shows that despite years in practice, experienced therapists do value input from colleagues. The difference between the novice and the expert lies in the types of supervision they need. The experienced therapists need supervision mostly for self-care and not for clinical supervisions. To be 'self-reflexive', a therapist needs to reflect on professional practice, which involves the metacognitive process or knowledge about the professional and personal. Critical reflection allows the therapist to place his or her self within the political-social context, which informs his or her identity. Thus, being reflexive allows the therapist to realise his or her strengths and limitations, which help in getting the care that the therapist needs. For example, therapists have also reported attending to their physical selves by eating a healthy diet, sleeping well, exercising regularly, and having physical contact with the people they love.

Norcross and Guy (2007) discussed in their book that how recurrent self-care themes from master therapists that they interviewed include getting ample sleep. The importance of sleep is crucial to restore energy and optimise potential. They further emphasised sleeping routines or sleeping hygiene to ensure that the mind and body receive ample rest. Therapists typically spend many hours sitting, either to attend to clients or to do other administrative tasks related to their practices. Furthermore, attending to clients also means that therapists are responding physically to their stories. Norcross and Guy (2007) stated that the body is the receiver. Often, when the stories are stressful, the listener will feel them.

Thus, the therapist absorbs the stories physically, and the body reacts to the stories through muscle tension. Hence, self-care entails body relaxation techniques that can include but are not limited to massage, sauna, tai-chi, and stretching.

Additionally, research has shown that regular short physical activities, such as walking in an accessible green space, provide wonders to the body and the mind. Green exercise helps to boost physical and mental health, particularly mood and self-esteem (Barton and Pretty, 2009). Thus, taking a short break by walking in a nearby green space might be another option that can be a part of self-care practice. Hegarty (2010), in his study among trainee counsellors and members of the scientific green care panel, found that participants' connection with nature helped their personal healing. The idea of nature as healer lies in its silence, calmness, and ability to provide calmness (Walsh, 2011), away from the hustles of noise and technology. Thus, therapists' awareness of the benefits of nature and its utilisation is suggested to be one of the ways to increase mental health. Therapists also reported that some factors that they used to care for their mental well-being include undergoing training, continuing education, and mindful awareness (Harrison and Westwood, 2009).

Personal therapy

Regardless of how therapists approach self-care, there is no denying that self-care should be part and parcel of best practices, specifically to ensure that therapists are continuously motivated to work towards the best interests of their clients. Several authors have shown the impact of personal therapy on therapists' professional lives (Williams et al., 2015; Bike et al., 2009; Williams et al., 2003; Street and Rivett, 1996). The experienced therapists in the study of Williams et al. (2003) reported that they managed the concerns that might affect their therapeutic sessions by seeking personal therapy, which they suggested was crucial to gaining self-knowledge and insight into their countertransference issues. I believe that personal therapy is important in one's development as a psychotherapist. The therapist is recommended to practise what he or she preaches. I benefitted from post-divorce therapy to understand and process what took place and learn how to move forward as a sole parent. Nevertheless, seeking therapy was not the norm in my culture; it was easier to seek therapy when I was in the West compared to when I returned to my home country. This is probably due to the strong stigma of a professional seeking mental health care and cultural issues revolving around confidentiality where gossip is part of the cultural practices. Perhaps it is just an illusion that therapists as professional mental health carers can manage their own issues themselves. My concern regarding privacy in my own culture is not unique, as Bearse et al. (2013) illustrated that privacy concerns may be an issue because of stigma. The fear of being seen in a therapist's office keeps some therapists from getting the help they need. This might relate to the concern of how their therapists might guard their confidentiality, as violation of privacy might cost these therapists their future work.

Despite the issues concerning confidentiality and privacy, it is important that the therapist is aware of when he or she is not able to be present to the clients, given that the self of the practitioner is part of the alliance equation. Norcross et al. (1988) conducted a national survey in the United States involving 234 psychologists, 104 psychiatrists, and 171 clinical social workers regarding their therapeutic processes and the outcomes of their personal psychotherapy experiences. Their findings showed that the majority of therapists sought therapy for personal reasons and reported positive results in their behaviours, cognitions, and emotions. Another example of the impact of personal therapy on a therapist's development is described by Macran et al. (1999), who interviewed seven psychotherapists in the UK. One of their findings illustrated that personal therapy allowed therapists to understand their roles as therapists, to be more empathic towards their clients, and to describe 'being human' or 'being themselves' (p. 423).

Considering the benefits of receiving personal therapy, a system needs to be in place for therapists to feel safe when asking for help, which very much relates to the idea of having a secure attachment style and the ability to be reflexive. Perhaps this can be embedded in the supervision process, and, thus, having someone not from the same agency as stressed by therapists in my study, might be something to consider. Exercise 6.8 is based on the work of Williams et al. (2015) in terms of bringing in a family member to a consultation meeting as part of training. This exercise can be done with a supervisor or a colleague.

Exercise 6.8 Bringing Your Family Member to Consultation

1. Who do you bring in with you?
2. Ask your family member to describe your role, in relation to the strengths and weaknesses in your family.
3. How do you feel hearing their descriptions about yourself?
4. Do you agree or disagree with the description provided by your family member? Explain.
5. What do you think of this exercise?

Consultation with family members has been reported to be beneficial for trainee therapists. They attributed the benefits to the richness of their learning experiences and their experience of being in the role of clients, which made them more sensitive towards their clients' feelings, and in acknowledging the importance of therapeutic alliance (Williams et al., 2015). Despite any ethical dilemmas about bringing one's family member into consultation, trainee therapists reported that the benefits outweigh the inevitable effect of family involvement. The participants reported that this experiential learning experience is far superior to other types of learning, such as clinical placement or academic learning (Williams et al., 2015).

It is worth noting that in the Williams et al. study, trainees whose spouses were also therapists benefitted the most from personal therapy, but other family members were less clear on the purpose of their involvement in therapy. They suggested that making family understand the meaning they bring into consultation, or the role they play, might ease the process, and provide better relational interaction for both the trainees and their family members.

The earlier chapters illustrated the impact that attachment as well as our family of origin have on the self. Thus, training should include attachment work focusing on repairing our own relationship challenges or ruptures, especially involving people close to us. This may constitute individual work or bringing family members to further explore the self of the therapist. Exercise 6.9 invites you to ponder on whether personal therapy may be one of the options that you may consider for your self-care.

Exercise 6.9 Your Thoughts on Personal Therapy

Personal therapy involves a lot of introspection and soul-searching work:

1. Do you think this may be one of the options for you?
2. If yes, discuss why. If no, discuss the pros and cons of getting personal therapy.

Practical strategies

Setting clear boundaries between one's personal and professional lives is one of the self-care strategies that therapists can utilise. Therapists must learn to be assertive and say 'no' to certain things that might not be beneficial for either their personal or professional lives. Having too much on one's plate can be taxing for therapists, whose job requires physical, mental, and emotional endurance and resilience. Setting limits includes avoiding dual relationships and recognising one's limitations as therapists (Harrison and Westwood, 2009). Therapists should realise that they are not responsible for making changes in clients' lives. Some strategies utilised by therapists in Harrison and Westwood's (2009) study include peer consultation; mindful attending to unresolved issues in order to process them and to achieve closure; personal rituals before and after work; taking time off work to travel; and consciously setting limits between their professional and personal spaces, such as not working on one's birthday.

Other strategies include cognitive restructuring. Norcross and Guy (2007), in their book *Leaving It at the Office: A Guide to Psychotherapist Self-Care,* stated that therapists probably accomplish more than they realise. Thus, therapists are advised to address any cognitive distortion they have by breaking down vague problems into workable parts. For example, therapists might think that they should undertake multiple tasks or take on many clients, and believe they will be seen as less of a therapist if they decide to say no. Thus, writing down actions or thoughts might help therapists to clarify things and serve as evidence that therapists have accomplished many tasks. This boosts morale and puts things into perspective and allows therapists to see clearly if they have been taking on more than they should. Furthermore, writing or journalling can be beneficial and therapeutic. I myself keep a gratitude journal to remind me of simple, daily, beautiful things that I tend to take for granted. I found this to be helpful and a mindful way for self-monitoring.

Furthermore, self-care strategies such as creative writing, journalling, reflecting, and engaging in advocacy work that promote engagement with others also promote reconstruction of new meaning (Bressi and Vaden, 2017), similar to reflexive practice in attachment. Bressi and Vaden (2017), in their work on reconsidering self-care, stated that self-care needs to include mechanisms for meaning-making and self-discovery. According to them, relational and recovery-orientation models produce change for both therapists and clients, in a 'bi-directional, co-constructed fashion' (p. 37). These models encourage practitioners to actively reflect on how their work with clients brings meaning to their lives. Thus, therapists' emotional distress should be normalised, and they should be empowered to see distress as a natural and an important part of their work with clients, as well as in terms of their personal development. They suggested activities that might work for therapists to reframe when confronted with conflict that stirs their own inner selves. The purpose of these activities is (p. 37):

- to cope with distress in the body and mind;
- to locate their own reactions as communications from clients or countertransference responses to clients;
- to offer opportunities for reflection on their own assumptions about clients and their own lives; and
- to avoid the use of affects and thoughts related to clients as the primary form of self-care or frame for use of self.

In bridging the gap: How do we learn reflexivity?

Self-care can only manifest when reflexivity is made possible. However, it can be difficult to learn reflexivity or reflect upon past experiences. We have to be cautioned to not equate being reflexive or recreating new narratives with throwing away our pain and past memories. In my experience that would be counterproductive. Therapists with secure attachment styles showed that they used their knowledge or past experiences in approaching their clients and practices and for overcoming biases. For example, one therapist realised when his past experience – having a complaining mother – might hinder his work. He said that he might not be objective when meeting such clients. Having a secure attachment style allowed this therapist to reflect on his experience and make a sound decision when his attachment insecurity is activated. Thus, we obtain knowledge or insight into our experiences when given the opportunity to reflect and to think about and feel, as well as act on, the experiences. This includes when reflecting on relationship dynamics, that is, the associated thoughts and feelings that help us to make sense of the situation and respond accordingly (Ruch, 2002). Exercise 6.10 below is based on Aponte and Carlsen (2009), who advocated that therapists in training should work on themselves and not let their personal issues get in the way of their therapeutic alliances. This exercise can be utilised in supervision with the support of the supervisor or a colleague.

Exercise 6.10 Meaning Making in Therapy

This exercise should be conducted once you have completed your session with clients:

1. Provide identifying information about your client.
2. State the reason the client is in therapy and whether this carries any personal meaning for you.
3. Describe your reaction to your clients and their reactions towards you.
4. Address the underlying issues that you think might contribute to how you view your clients or their issues.
5. Discuss your plan on how to address your personal challenges.

The Aponte model encourages therapists to examine their personal issues and family histories. According to Aponte and Carlsen, the personal and the professional self are connected and displayed in the work that therapists do with clients. It is probably apt to conclude that in practice and in dealing with human emotions, there is no black-and-white approach but rather an array of approaches. The therapist is building the bridge between the personal and the work that they do. Hence, self-reflexivity deals with the 'greyness' or the uncertain nature of the self and practice, as anything can be thrown at the practitioner. Ruch (2002) further elaborated that reflective practice enables the integration of the professional and the personal selves. This resolves the conflicts of a separable identity and provides intellectual understanding and emotional awareness that inform thoughts, decisions, and actions. It allows us to understand the contribution of our personal knowledge to practice and vice versa.

Thus, utilising the self of the therapist and being reflexive requires that therapists involve themselves in how their training is shaped. Similar to treating clients as being expert in their own issues, training centres should involve therapists in shaping their training, as therapists' input ensures that their voices are being heard. This includes taking into account research findings as they provide us with the initial landscape of the scenarios on the ground. The integration of research into practice was probably not a general inclination of all practitioners. Despite the move for counselling and psychotherapy training in addressing the theory and skills of psychotherapeutic research, trainees often focus on therapeutic skills in the therapy room and look to supervisors to increase their skills. They, however, tend to be less focused on building their capacity as '*reflective practitioners grounded in research, which is necessary for them to function autonomously as professionals*' (Sennett in Wheeler and Elliot, 2008, p. 133). Therefore, reflexive practice is not a one-way process where knowledge and experience are being imparted from the therapist to the client or from the supervisor to the trainee. It is a cyclical process, in which everyone is involved. Hence, for us to be more inclusive, the process of reflexivity is a challenge for everyone in the therapeutic room.

The importance of practitioners involving themselves in research reflects the scientist-practitioner model (Crane et al., 2002). Crane suggests that, within the scientist-practitioner model, therapists should be immersed in both research and clinical skills (Crane and McArthur, 2002).

Reflexivity bridges the gap between research and practice, between clients and therapists, as well as between trainees and supervisors, if each of the individuals reflects on and is mindful of how each contributes to the present scenario. Therapists – like training centres or supervisors – have the ability to create a secure base for clients or trainees to explore their issues. What is reflexivity then? The concept of reflexive practice is associated with the work of Schon (1991) who proposed the inability of the technical/rational approach to provide solutions for a professional problem-solving framework. The technical-rationality approach views the application of scientific theory and technique as a method for solving our daily problems. This creates a practical tension in solving our daily problems that are often not as straightforward as they seem and cannot be solved by adhering only to standards and regulations. Professional practice mostly utilises complex nontechnical, nonlinear, and non-rational processes. It very much relies on our creativity, innovative capabilities, and insights.

Thus, the process of acquiring knowledge in practice cannot rely solely on a rigid standard of technical or rational mode. Schon's reflective-practice paradigm acknowledges that knowledge and action are not necessarily connected. The emergence of knowledge can, however, occur simultaneously with action, through reflexive processing. This process involves bringing to consciousness 'the tacit knowing – the intuitive know-how – which guides professional skill' (Papell and Skolnik, 1992). It is often a messy practice that emerges from facing a puzzling situation and in trying to understand where the practitioner considers various factors, such as their actions and roles, in which intuition, past experience, and theory are utilised in this reflection-in-action process. Knowledge in action is said to develop when such mental processes are accompanied by actions, words or concepts to explain the know-how or tacit knowledge (Papell and Skolnik, 1992).

Therefore, for reflexivity to take place, we need to consider therapists' voices and their needs, because they are the experts. Every competent practitioner can recognise an issue or an array of symptoms that lead to the conclusion of a particular phenomenon or diagnosis. At times, the practitioner cannot provide a complete picture, and, in their daily practice, they make numerous judgements of things that cannot be ascertained because of inadequate criteria. Thus, practitioners always display skills that cannot be explained through rules and procedures when being confronted with an issue, and though they might use research-based theories and techniques, the practitioner very much relies on their tacit recognitions, judgements, and skills concerning what they are used to (Schon, 1991). This relates to the interviews where reflexivity, as shown by the depth of therapists' narratives, suggests the need for therapists with various attachment styles to delve into the self of the therapists through a continuous self-reflexive process. A reflective practitioner or therapist then is someone who is self-aware and adaptable. He or she is able to evaluate each situation and process through critical reflections and not adhere to rigid formulas in problem solving. Nonetheless, expert and novice practitioners differ in how they use manuals or follow procedures. The experts, due to their experience, have the luxury of being selective and probably skip some parts in the manual due to their expert intuition that guides their practices (Greenhalgh et al. in Stratton and Hanks, 2016).

Additionally, Boud (1999) explained in his paper that the argument regarding incorporating reflexivity in practice is not whether reflexivity should occur but how it should be formulated as part of a formal curriculum. In teaching reflexivity, as with many therapeutic practices in which trainees are encouraged to keep learning journals or other methods to increase reflexivity, Boud (1999) reiterates that the issues lie not within the methods used but in how they are being utilised, as described below:

- ➢ The following method involves a set of guidelines concerning how to approach an issue, such as to reflect by numbers. I must admit that, at times, I fall into such a reductionistic manner in approaching an issue, especially when time is a factor. Deep reflection cannot occur when we have to reassess an experience or a problem by evaluating it through stages.
- ➢ Reflection without learning is when time is given, but it is insufficient for reflection to occur.
- ➢ Intellectualising reflection is when we treat reflection as a purely cognitive process and do not take into account the element of feelings and emotions.
- ➢ Inappropriate disclosure can occur when we expect therapists and trainees to reveal personal details of the reflection of an incident.

Jensen (2016) further emphasised the circular concept of resonance in which the therapist, the therapist's clients, and the therapist's personal life play a role in the way therapy is conducted. Diverse social constructions of the self and the norms that govern the self, such as our cultural or religious backgrounds, may impact on the therapeutic alliance. Thus, the author suggested that therapists should reflect on what they learn and bring home from their work as therapists, as well as what they bring into therapy from their personal life experiences.

Additionally, we can learn reflexivity in the supervisory process as supervision is an experiential learning involving two models (Carroll, 2010): (1) the After Action Review (AAR) devised by the American military, and (2) the Experiential Learning Cycle (ELC) developed by Kolb (in Kolb and Kolb, 2009). The AAR basically reviews the process from planning (what we set out to do), the pros and cons of the actual event, and the learning aspect post-event, which include thinking about doing things differently.

The ELC involves reflecting, learning, and applying what has been learned to future situations. Critical reflection involves emotional and cognitive experiences, and often the activation to reflect manifests in several ways (Carroll, 2010):

- facing a dilemma where we start to question or rethink our ideas and theories;
- having strong emotional responses or feelings that make us think and rethink about the situation;
- discovering our assumptions and the meaning we attach to these assumptions, which are often based on our values, life experiences, and thinking;
- feelings of restlessness or dissatisfaction with things that we get, receive, or inherit from others;
- realising that we are unauthentic, living in other people's values or scripts; and
- realising that there are other psychological truths besides our own.

This process allows us to reflect on our own assumptions and values that may interfere in our work as practitioners. Critical reflection involves being mindful of our experience, thinking, and being aware of the intersections between race, religion, ethnicity, sexual orientation, and other differences that we bring with us in our work with clients. Earlier, we discussed the difficulty of group work when doing reflexive practice (Lennie, 2007). This probably relates to the nature of group exercises where we have many therapists and one supervisor. Thus, most likely, therapists in group therapy, despite their similarities as therapists, may only reflect on the rudimentary processes of therapeutic work and will not delve further into the impact of their work on the selves. This is especially so when such disclosure may create discomfort and challenge the therapist's thinking and way of doing things.

Nonetheless, the benefits of reflexive practice or self-awareness training are well documented (Pieterse et al., 2013), especially in personal therapy. Reflecting on my own training, I had the luxury of both group and individual supervisions. Nevertheless, both types of supervision only involved matters concerning skills and client issues. Back then, we did not discuss the self of the person conducting therapy or the impact of the therapeutic alliance, let alone the social impact of the environment or events such as 9/11 on the therapists.

However, it is important to note that the teaching and practice of reflexive practice involve multiple ethical issues, such as confidentiality, rights to privacy, informed consent, and professional relationships. It is a powerful tool that can have a profound emotional impact (Finlay, 2008), and, potentially, without supervision, can be detrimental to the person's reflecting. Exercise 6.11 invites you to reflect on the ethical issues you might encounter when working with reflexive practice.

Exercise 6.11 Ethical Issues in Reflexive Practice

1. What will you do to minimise ethical issues, such as breach of confidentiality or undisclosed information that may hinder your therapeutic growth?
2. Do you agree that cultural and personal risks are involved in reflexive practice? Discuss.

It is important for educators and supervisors to assess each trainee therapist individually, as every individual's experience is different. There is no one-size-fits-all model; hence, as discussed earlier, personal therapy or closed small-group supervision may be among the ways of approaching the teaching-learning of reflexive practice. However, group supervision may only work for some therapists, as, most likely, therapists or trainees may refrain from divulging in self-disclosure or in matters impacting the selves. For reflexive practice to work, individuals should be provided with support to process their experience, feelings, and the impact of their new-found awareness.

Do you agree with Finlay (2008) that reflexive practice should be applied selectively, taught sensitively, and generally used with care? Reflexive practice involves developmental readiness on the part of the therapist or trainee, which differentiates between a novice and an expert therapist. Reflection can be less effective when attachment insecurity is activated or there is a perceived threat. A 'safe' space requires alliance building between the therapist and the supervisor, colleague, or mentor. A training centre should address this issue and allow the therapist or trainee therapist to critically analyse, reflect, and form meaning of their encounters with clients and supervisors.

Additionally, supervisors and training centres should prepare therapists to be relevant for the future as the world becomes more complex with an array of cases to be used in training and create reflective moments on the job, especially for novices to become aware of their own psychological truth and the absolute truth. The chapter on attachment shows that attachment can be developmentally based or biologically based. Thus, training for future therapists and therapists in continuous professional development should involve multidisciplinary healthcare perspectives and an understanding of how to look at the self, and the intersections between our biology, genealogy, psychology, culture, religion, sexuality, social ties, and environment.

Reflexive practitioners engage in continuous critical self-reflection, which brings us to the idea of the 'wounded healer' (Bennet, 1984). Potentially, the wounded healer can be the 'best' healer depending on whether the wound, physical or psychological, is attended to. An unattended wound or trauma can resurface in many forms that may hinder or sever the therapeutic alliance. Some authors perceive woundedness as a continuum process (Zerubavel and Wright, 2012; Cvetovac and

Adame, 2017) that enfolds the human experience. Nobody is immune to being wounded, but wounded healers have the capacity to become great clinicians if they manage to integrate their experiences into practice (Graves, 2008). The therapists in the study of Cvetovac and Adame (2017) reported the culture of the profession that made self-disclosing harder. This is due to the stigma and fear of professional repercussions from colleagues and supervisors. However, a supportive relationship with their supervisors helped to mediate the risk, which shows the importance of supervisory support in deactivating the negative emotion that may trigger attachment insecurity.

Thus, if we are to promote self-reflexivity in practice, training, and supervision, there are several best practices that we need to consider. Some suggestions on practice include the following (Rhodes et al., 2011; Graves, 2008; Boud, 2001; Boud, 1999; Papell and Skolnik, 1992):

- Therapists, supervisors, and training centres need to establish ground rules for therapeutic sessions and training. This should be mutually agreeable to the involved parties and open to challenges.
- There must be flexibility in the viewing structure and processes including removing barriers for better participation. If aspects of the self of the practitioner are barriers to delivering better services, then one of the ways to enhance participation is through training on the self of the therapist, such as knowing your attachment styles and the family of origin.
- Therapists, supervisors, and training centres can ensure a supportive environment for best practices to occur, such as access to regular individual and group supervision, time to reflect, adequate support, resources, opportunities, and methods for reflection. This includes developing the skills of critical analysis and considering the context of reflection. Any reflection should be nurtured naturally, in order to motivate therapists to continue to engage in reflexive work. Opening a can of worms should involve transparency on the part of the training centres and supervisors in providing adequate support to process the experience, especially when facing upsetting outcomes.
- Other tools include using critical incidents, reflective dialogical exercises with mentors or peers, role play, and practical exercises. Critical

incidents, such as the events of 9/11 and their aftermath, evoke powerful feelings for those directly or indirectly experiencing them. Writing up the incident and subsequent analysis helps to situate the event within wider contextual issues, such as geopolitics, and the social impact that such tragedies hold for oneself, and for the countless who have lost their loved ones.

- On a micro-level, reflective practice can occur by utilising process recording. This is a method used to record the verbatim accounts between the practitioner and the client in order to encourage the reflective process. This method has been used in many classrooms and in fieldwork where the practitioner has to record his or her thoughts prior to engagement with a client, to record what transpired, to write down a formulation account based on what has transpired in the engagement, and to suggest possible intervention strategies. My own clinical training utilised process recording in which client engagements were recorded, and a verbatim word-for-word transcription of what transpired during engagement, including my own observations were carefully noted. This process was then translated into a case formulation describing in detail a client's presentations in various aspects, such as cognitively and intrapsychically; behavioural, family, and intergenerational issues; strengths and weaknesses; network and support structure; and my own observations. An intervention strategy was then developed based on the case formulation (University Centre for the Child and Family in Yusof, 2005). This method, although useful for training, might be a challenge to utilise in a working environment where time is a factor. Nevertheless, this tool might help therapists to increase reflexivity. Other useful tools include reviewing video recordings of sessions, which can assist therapists to reflect on their strengths and weaknesses in sessions and determine whether attachment or other factors are intertwined in their work as therapists.

- Journal writing is also a process that reflective practice can enhance. According to Boud (2001), journal writing can be a form of self-expression, a record of events, or a form of therapy. It can be utilised as a device to record events and experiences and to extract meaning from them. In journal writing, the practitioner uses the unprocessed, raw material of experience and engages with it in order to understand what has transpired. Thus, reflection is a process of turning experience into learning. The process of making sense of these experiences will result in building a foundation for new learning to occur. It is important to note that for this process to work, the practitioner should write 'honestly', exploring uncertain and perplexing events, which are often messy, and unknown to the writer. Although journal writing can be empowering as a tool for reflexivity, it should not be used in assessment as this might activate attachment insecurities, which might hinder a therapist's development.

- Additionally, Ruch (2002) proposed co-working as a way for practitioners to develop self-reflexivity. This relates closely to approaches in family therapy when practitioners work in a team and split their work between working directly with the family or becoming the observer. The observer will have the opportunity to provide feedback of his or her observation to the family, which might be useful to the therapist who works directly with the family and to the family members themselves. Reflection allows practitioners to support each other, reflect upon their practices, and discuss any emerging countertransference issues. However, co-working or a reflecting team seems to focus on the family, and not on the family and the therapeutic process. Therefore, an additional tool, such as a log book or a diary, might be useful for self-reflexivity once feedback is received from the co-worker.
- Besides co-working, the therapists in my study valued group supervision as an opportunity for reflection. Group supervision provides a space for practitioners to come together to discuss issues related to their clients, as well as personal issues that might affect their practice. The discussion of practice provides support and enhances transparency, which allows greater accountability, as it can become a check-and-balance mechanism for therapists to identify and correct assumptions and biases. Nevertheless, this might only be suitable for experienced therapists, as novice therapists may be unable to self-reflect or self-disclose in a group.
- Encourage continuous supervision as part of self-development throughout a therapist's career.
- Training should utilise various teaching-learning methods to acknowledge the experience of woundedness as part of the human experience, such as using cases, therapists' excerpts concerning their personal

development, books, poetry, or assignments that promote self-reflexivity. For example, in teaching foundation social work practice, I utilise a YouTube video to reflect on the concept of empathy. This video illustrates that everyone has issues – bad and good. As future practitioners, this allows students to reflect on and understand the wound of others and the importance of being attuned to their own reaction. Future training may include simulation exercises to practice and reflect on the ways of engaging and doing things. Even though human contact is crucial in working with clients, I suggest that in the era of Industry 4.0 and virtual-reality, exercises mirroring contacts with clients, displaying several case scenarios, such as working with hard-to-reach populations or children, may be worth exploring. This however, needs further research, and, most likely, might benefit a novice practitioner or a trainee therapist more than an experienced therapist.

Exercise 6.12 Self-Reflexivity in Practice

Other than the one listed above, there are many ways to develop or enhance self-reflexivity in practice:

- What methods have you utilised?
- What are your thoughts regarding them?

The therapists I interviewed showed that the self and the knowledge we have can be a powerful tool in guiding practices. There is also the element of open versus closed knowledge (Thompson and Thompson, 2008), where therapists with secure attachment styles utilised open knowledge of the self, in which they realised and acknowledged how the selves affected practices by being informed about their experiences. They were also sensitive to realising their limitations that might hinder alliance building. This open knowledge makes therapists more creative, such as using humour, ethics, and accountability, in challenging the assumptions they have. Closed knowledge, on the other hand, will make therapists uninformed about the aspect of the self that can be limiting to practice; therapists can be potentially insensitive to surroundings when engaging in daily routines, particularly when their attachment insecurities are activated. By being sensitive to their own selves, therapists will be in tune with their values, emotions, and actions and can be their own internal auditor to realise when they can no longer be the anchor to their clients and seek help from supervisors and colleagues.

This writing process is a journey, as I took a year off work to focus on writing and reflecting to allow all the joy and ghosts of past experiences to emerge. In connecting the dots, I understand that past experiences, the good and the bad, are important to facilitate the present experience and shape the future. It is challenging to admit to oneself the unconscious biases and ideas that one has in building alliances. However, this is what makes us human, and, as helping professionals, we need to take a closer look and constantly challenge our biases, assumptions, and ideas. Self-reflexivity can only manifest in a safe space analogous to the ability of a therapist providing a safe space for a client to explore his or her own issues. Similarly, supervisors and training centres need to provide a safe space for alliances to develop. The alliance, which consists of engagement, emotional connection, and a shared sense of purpose, can only grow when therapists understand themselves better.

Chapter summary

- A supervisor provides a similar role to that of a therapist to a client. A supervisory session has the potential to provide safety for supervisees with different attachment styles to be open and vulnerable to discuss in-session or issues that help or hinder therapeutic work.
- Supervision is important for the growth and development of therapists.
- Supervision is especially important to lone therapists.
- Supervision should be performed by a supervisor employed outside the supervisee's agency.
- Self-reflexivity and self-care are integral aspects of practice. These two elements should be incorporated and emphasised in training and supervision.

References

ACKERMAN, S. J. & HILSENROTH, M. J. 2003. A review of therapist characteristics and techniques positively impacting the therapeutic alliance. *Clinical Psychology Review*, 23, 1–33.

AINSWORTH, M. D. S. 1989. Attachments beyond infancy. *American Psychologist*, 44, 709–716.

AINSWORTH, M. D. S., BLEHAR, M. C., WATERS, E. & WALL, S. 1978. *Patterns of attachment: A psychological study of the strange situation*. New Jersey: Lawrence Erlbaum Associates.

ALLMAN, J. M., WATSON, K. K., TETREAULT, N. A. & HAKEEM, A. Y. 2005. Intuition and autism: A possible role for von Economo neurons. *Trends in Cognitive Sciences*, 9, 367–373.

ALVES DE OLIVEIRA, J. & VANDENBERGHE, L. 2009. Upsetting experiences for the therapist in-session: How they can be dealt with and what they are good for. *Journal of Psychotherapy Integration*, 19, 231–245.

ANDERSON, H. & SWIM, S. 1995. Supervision as collaborative conversation: Connecting the voices of supervisor and supervisee. *Journal of Systemic Therapies*, 14, 1–13.

APONTE, H. J. 1998. Love, the spiritual wellspring of forgiveness: An example of spirituality in therapy. *Journal of Family Therapy*, 20, 37–58.

APONTE, H. J. & CARLSEN, J. C. 2009. An instrument for person-of-the-therapist supervision. *Journal of Marital and Family Therapy*, 35, 395–405.

BACHELOR, A. 1995. Clients' perception of the therapeutic alliance: A qualitative analysis. *Journal of Counseling Psychology*, 42, 323–337.

BARTHOLOMEW, K. & HOROWITZ, L. M. 1991. Attachment styles among young adults: A test of a four-category model. *Journal of Personality and Social Psychology*, 61, 226–244.

BARTON, J. & PRETTY, J. 2009. What is the best dose of nature and green exercise for improving mental health? A multi-study analysis. *Environmental Science & Technology*, 44, 3947–3955.

BEARSE, J. L., MCMINN, M. R., SEEGOBIN, W. & FREE, K. 2013. Barriers to psychologists seeking mental health care. *Professional Psychology: Research and Practice*, 44, 150–157.

BECK, M., FRIEDLANDER, M. L. & ESCUDERO, V. 2006. Three perspectives on clients' experiences of the therapeutic alliance: A discovery-oriented investigation. *Journal of Marital and Family Therapy*, 32, 355–368.

BEDI, R. P., DAVIS, M. D. & WILLIAMS, M. 2005. Critical incidents in the formation of therapeutic alliance from the client's perspective. *Psychotherapy: Theory, Research, Practice, Training*, 42, 311–323.

BENNET, G. 1984. The wounded healer in the twentieth century: Re-evaluation of an ancient idea. *British Journal of Holistic Medicine*, 1, 127–130.

BEUTLER, L. E., CRAGO, M. & ARIZMENDI, T. G. 1986. Research on therapist variables in psychotherapy. *In:* GARFIELD, S. L. & BERGIN, A. E. (eds.) *Handbook of psychotherapy and behavior change*. New York: John Wiley & Sons.

BIKE, D. H., NORCROSS, J. C. & SCHATZ, D. M. 2009. Processes and outcomes of psychotherapists' personal therapy: Replication and extension 20 years later. *Psychotherapy: Theory, Research, Practice, Training*, 46, 19–31.

BLACK, S., HARDY, G., TURPIN, G. & PARRY, G. 2005. Self-reported attachment styles and therapeutic orientation of therapists and their relationship with reported general alliance quality and problems in therapy. *Psychology and Psychotherapy: Theory, Research and Practice*, 78, 363–377.

BLATT, S. J., SANISLOW III, C. A., ZUROFF, D. C. & PILKONIS, P. A. 1996. Characteristics of effective therapists: Further analyses of data from the National Institute of Mental Health Treatment of Depression Collaborative Research program. *Journal of Consulting and Clinical Psychology*, 64, 1276–1284.

BORDIN, E. S. 1979. The generalizability of the psychoanalytic concept of the working alliance. *Psychotherapy: Theory, Research, Practice, Training*, 16, 252–260.

BOUD, D. 1999. Avoiding the traps: Seeking good practice in the use of self assessment and reflection in professional courses. *Social Work Education*, 18, 121–132.

BOUD, D. 2001. Using journal writing to enhance reflective practice. *New Directions for Adult and Continuing Education*, 90, 9–17.

BOURGEOIS, L., SABOURIN, S. & WRIGHT, J. 1990. Predictive validity of therapeutic alliance in group marital therapy. *Journal of Consulting and Clinical Psychology*, 58, 608–613.

BOWDEN, E. M. & JUNG-BEEMAN, M. 2003. Aha! Insight experience correlates with solution activation in the right hemisphere. *Psychonomic Bulletin & Review*, 10, 730–737.

BOWLBY, J. 1973. *Attachment and loss: Separation, anxiety and anger*. London: The Hogath Press.

BOWLBY, J. 1980. *Attachment and loss: Loss, sadness and depression*. London: The Hogarth Press.

BOWLBY, J. 1988a. *A secure base: Clinical applications of attachment theory.* London: Routledge.

BOWLBY, J. 1988b. *A secure base: Parent-child attachment and healthy human development.* New York: Basic Books.

BRENNAN, K. A., CLARK, C. L. & SHAVER, P. R. 1998. Self-report measurement of adult romantic attachment: An integrative overview. *In:* SIMPSON, J. A. & RHOLES, W. S. (eds.) *Attachment theory and close relationship.* New York: Guilford Press.

BRESSI, S. K. & VADEN, E. R. 2017. Reconsidering self care. *Clinical Social Work Journal,* 45, 33–38.

BRETHERTON, I. 1985. Attachment theory: Retrospect and prospect. *Monographs of the Society for Research in Child Development,* 50, 3–35.

BRETHERTON, I. & MUNHOLLAND, K. A. 1999. Internal working models in attachment relationships: A construct revisited. *In:* CASSIDY, J. & SHAVER, P. R. (eds.) *Handbook of attachment: Theory, research and clinical applications.* New York: Guilford Press.

BROWN, B. (2012). *Daring greatly: How the courage to be vulnerable transforms the way we live, love, parent and lead.* London: Portfolio Penguin.

BROWN, P. D. & O'LEARY, D. K. 2000. Therapeutic alliance: Predicting continuance and success in group treatment for spouse abuse. *Journal of Consulting and Clinical Psychology,* 68, 340–345.

BURNHAM, J. 2012. Developments in social GGRRAAACCEEESSS: Visible-invisible and voiced-unvoiced. *In:* KRAUSE, I.-B. (ed.) *Culture and reflexivity in systemic psychotherapy.* London: Karnac.

BYNG-HALL, J. 1995. Creating a secure family base: Some implications of attachment theory for family therapy. *Family Process,* 34, 45–58.

BYNG-HALL, J. 2008. The crucial roles of attachment in family therapy. *Journal of Family Therapy,* 30, 129–146.

CARROLL, M. 2010. Supervision: Critical reflection for transformational learning (Part 2). *The Clinical Supervisor,* 29, 1–19.

COMBS, A. W. 1989. *A theory of therapy: Guidelines for counseling practice.* California: Sage.

CRANE, R. D. & MCARTHUR, H. J. 2002. Meeting the needs of evidence-based practice in family therapy: Developing the Scientist-Practitioner model. *Journal of Family Therapy,* 24, 113–124.

CRANE, R. D., WAMPLER, K. S., SPRENKLE, D. H., SANDBERG, J. G. & HOVESTADT, A. J. 2002. The scientist-practitioner model in marriage and family therapy doctoral programs: Current status. *Journal of Marital and Family Therapy,* 28, 75–83.

CUTCLIFFE, J. R. 2003. Reconsidering reflexivity: Introducing the case for intellectual entrepreneurship. *Qualitative Health Research,* 13, 136–148.

CVETOVAC, M. E. & ADAME, A. L. 2017. The wounded therapist: Understanding the relationship between personal suffering and clinical practice. *The Humanistic Psychologist*, 45, 348–366.

DALLOS, R. & VETERE, A. 2009. *Systemic therapy and attachment narratives: Applications in a range of clinical settings*. London: Routledge.

DAVIDSON, R. J. & MCEWAN, B. S. 2012. Social influences on neuroplasticity: Stress and interventions to promote well-being. *Nature Neuroscience*, 15, 689–695.

DEUTSCH, C. J. 1985. A survey of therapists' personal problems and treatment. *Professional Psychology: Research and Practice*, 16, 305–315.

DIENER, M. J. & MONROE, J. M. 2011. The relationship between adult attachment style and therapeutic alliance in individual psychotherapy: A meta-analytic review. *Psychotherapy*, 48, 237–248.

DOLAN, R. T., ARNKOFF, D. B. & GLASS, C. R. 1993. Client attachment style and the psychotherapist's personal stance. *Psychotherapy*, 30, 408–412.

DONATI, M. & WATTS, M. 2005. Personal development in counsellor training: Towards a clarification of inter-related concepts. *British Journal of Guidance & Counselling*, 33, 475–484.

DOZIER, M., CUE, K. L. & BARNETT, L. 1994. Clinicians as caregivers: Role of attachment organization in treatment. *Journal of Consulting and Clinical Psychology*, 62, 793–800.

DOZIER, M. & TYRRELL, C. 1998. The role of attachment in therapeutic relationships. *In:* SIMPSON, J. A. & RHOLES, S. W. (eds.) *Attachment theory and close relationships*. New York: Guilford Press.

DUNKLE, J. L. & FRIEDLANDER, M. L. 1996. Contribution of therapist experience and personal characteristics to the working alliance. *Journal of Counseling Psychology*, 43, 456–460.

ESCUDERO, V., FRIEDLANDER, M. L., VARELA, N. & ABASCAL, A. 2008. Observing the therapeutic alliance in family therapy: Associations with participants' perceptions and therapeutic outcomes. *Journal of Family Therapy*, 30, 194–214.

FARBER, B. A., LIPPERT, R. A. & NEVAS, D. B. 1995. The therapist as attachment figure. 32, 204–212.

FARBER, B. A., MANEVICH, I., METZGER, J. & SAYPOL, E. 2005. Choosing psychotherapy as a career: Why did we cross that road?. *Jounal of Clinical Psychology*, 61, 1009–1031.

FARBER, B. A. & METZGER, J. A. 2009. The therapist as a secure base. *In:* OBEGI, J. H. & BERANT, E. (eds.) *Attachment theory and research in clinical social work with adults*. New York: Guilford Press.

FINK, A., GRABNER, R. H., GEBAUER, D., REISHOFER, G., KOSCHUTNIG, K. & EBNER, F. 2010. Enhancing creativity by means of cognitive stimulation: Evidence from an fMRI study. *NeuroImage*, 52, 1687–1695.

FINLAY, L. 2008. Reflecting on 'reflective practice'. *PBPL CETL*. The Open University: Practice-based Professional Learning Centre.

FONAGY, P., GERGELY, G., JURIST, E. L. & TARGET, M. 2007. *Affect regulation, mentalization and the development of the self.* London: Karnac (Books) Ltd.

FONAGY, P., STEELE, M., STEELE, H., MORAN, G. S. & HIGGITT, A. C. 1991. The capacity for understanding mental states: The reflective self in parent and child and its significance for security of attachment. *Infant Mental Health Journal*, 12, 201–218.

FONAGY, P. & TARGET, M. 1997. Attachment and reflective function: Their role in self-organization. *Development and Psychopathology*, 9, 679–700.

FRALEY, C. R., WALLER, N. G. & BRENNAN, K. A. 2000. An item response theory analysis of self-report measures of adult attachment. *Journal of Personality and Social Psychology*, 78, 350–365.

FRAWLEY O'DEA, M. G. 2003. When the trauma is terrorism and the therapist is traumatised too: Working as an analyst since 9/11. *Psychoanalytic Perspectives*, 1, 67–89.

FRIEDLANDER, M. L., ESCUDERO, V. & HEATHERINGTON, L. 2006. *Therapeutic alliance in couple and family therapy*. Washington DC: American Psychological Association.

FRIEDLANDER, M. L., ESCUDERO, V., HEATHERINGTON, L., DEIHL, L., FIELD, N., LEHMAN, P., MCKEE, M. & CUTTING, M. 2005. System for Observing Family Therapy Alliances (Training Manual).

GARLAND, E. L. & HOWARD, M. O. 2009. Neuroplasticity, psychosocial genomics, and the biopsychosocial paradigm in the 21st century. *Health & Social Work*, 34, 191–199.

GASTON, L., THOMPSON, L., GALLAGHER, D., COURNOYER, L.-G. & GAGNON, R. 1998. Alliance, technique, and their interactions in predicting outcome of behavioral, cognitive, and brief dynamic therapy. *Psychotherapy Research*, 8, 190–209.

GLEBOVA, T., BARTLE-HARING, S., GANGAMMA, R., KNERR, M., DELANEY, R. O., MEYER, K., MCDOWELL, T., ADKINS, K. & GRAFSKY, E. 2010. Therapeutic alliance and progress in couple therapy: Multiple perspectives. *Journal of Family Therapy*, 33, 42–65.

GRABNER, R. H., FINK, A. & NEUBAUER, A. C. 2007. Brain correlates of self-rated originality of ideas: Evidence from event-related power and phase-locking changes in the EEG. *Behavioural Neuroscience*, 121, 224–230.

GRAVES, L. 2008. Teaching the wounded healer. *Medical Teacher*, 30, 217–219.

HARRISON, R. L. & WESTWOOD, M. J. 2009. Preventing vicarious traumatization of mental health therapists: Identifying protective practices. *Psychotherapy: Theory, Research, Practice, Training*, 46, 203–219.

HAZAN, C. & SHAVER, P. 1987. Romantic love conceptualized as an attachment process. *Journal of Personality and Social Psychology*, 52, 511–524.
HEDGES, F. 2010. *Reflexivity in therapeutic practice*. England: Palgrave Macmillan.
HEGARTY, J. R. 2010. Out of the consulting room and into the woods? Experiences of nature-connectedness and self-healing. *European Journal of Ecopsychology*, 1, 64–84.
HERSOUG, A. G., HOGLEND, P., MONSEN, J. T. & HAVIK, O. E. 2001. Quality of working alliance in psychotherapy. *Journal of Psychotherapy Practice Research*, 10, 205–216.
HOFFMAN, L. 1985. Beyond power and control: Toward a 'second order' family systems therapy. *Family Systems Medicine*, 3, 381–396.
HORVATH, A. O. & GREENBERG, L. S. 1989. Development and validation of the Working Alliance Inventory. *Journal of Counseling Psychology*, 36, 223–233.
HORVATH, A. O. & SYMONDS, B. D. 1991. Relation between working alliance and outcome in psychotherapy: A meta-analysis. *Journal of Counseling Psychology*, 38, 139–149.
HOWE, D. 2011. *Attachment across the lifecourse: A brief introduction*. London: Palgrave Macmillan.
JENNINGS, L., GOH, M., SKOVHOLT, T. M., HANSON, M. & BANERJEE-STEVENS, D. 2003. Multiple factors in the development of the expert counselor and therapist. *Journal of Career Development*, 30, 59–72.
JENSEN, P. 2016. Mind the map. *In:* VETERE, A. & STRATTON, P. (eds.) *Interacting selves*. Oxon: Routledge.
JOHNSON, L. N. & WRIGHT, D. W. 2002. Revisiting Bordin's theory on the therapeutic alliance: Implications for family therapy. *Contemporary Family Therapy*, 24, 257–269.
JOHNSON, S. M. & TALITMAN, E. 1997. Predictors of success in emotionally focused marital therapy. *Journal of Marital and Family Therapy*, 23, 135–152.
JUNG-BEEMAN, M., BOWDEN, E. M., HABERMAN, J., FRYMIARE, J. L., ARAMBEL-LIU, S., GREENBLATT, R., REBER, P. J. & KOUNIOS, J. 2004. Neural activity when people solve verbal problems with insight. *PLoS Biology*, 2, 500–510.
KARAMAT ALI, R. & BACHICHA, D. L. 2012. Systemic supervision practices compared: A closer look at 'reflection' and 'self ' in multisystemic therapy and family therapy supervision. *Clinical Child Psychology and Psychiatry*, 17, 192–197.
KARVER, M. S., HANDELSMAN, J. B., FIELDS, S. & BICKMAN, L. 2006. Meta-analysis of therapeutic relationship variables in youth and family therapy: The evidence for different relationship variables in the child and adolescent treatment outcome literature. *Clinical Psychology Review*, 26, 50–65.

KNOBLOCH-FEDDERS, L. M., PINSOF, W. M. & MANN, B. J. 2007. Therapeutic alliance and treatment progress in couple psychotherapy. *Journal of Marital and Family Therapy*, 33, 245–257.

KOLB, B. 1995. *Brain plasticity and behavior*. Hillsdale, NJ: Lawrence Erlbaum Associates, Inc.

KOLB, A. Y. & KOLB, D. A. 2009. A dynamic holistic approach to management learning, education and development. *In:* ARMSTRONG, S. J. & FUKAMI, C. V. (eds.) *Past, present and future perspectives of management learning, education and development*. London: Sage.

KOLB, B. & GIBB, R. 2011. Brain plasticity and behaviour in the developing brain. *Journal of Canadian Academy of Child Adolescent Psychiatry*, 20, 265–276.

KRUPNICK, J. L., SOTSKY, S. M., SIMMENS, S., MOYER, J., ELKIN, I., WATKINS, J. & PILKONIS, P. A. 1996. The role of the therapeutic alliance in psychotherapy and pharmachotherapy outcome: Findings in the National Institute of Mental Health Treatment of Depression Collaborative Research Program. *Journal of Consulting and Clinical Psychology*, 64, 532–539.

LAMBERT, S. F. & LAWSON, G. 2013. Resilience of professional counselors following Hurricanes Katrina and Rita. *Journal of Counseling and Development: JCD*, 91, 261–268.

LEIPER, R. & CASARES, P. 2000. An investigation of the attachment organization of clinical psychologists and its relationship to clinical practice. *British Journal of Medical Psychology*, 73, 449–464.

LENNIE, C. 2007. The role of personal development groups in counsellor training: Understanding factors contributing to self-awareness in the personal development group. *British Journal of Guidance & Counselling*, 35, 115–129.

LEVINE, S. S. 2007. Nothing but the truth: Self-disclosure, self-revelation, and the persona of the analyst. *Journal of the American Psychoanalytic Association*, 55, 81–104.

MACRAN, S., STILES, W. B. & SMITH, J. A. 1999. How does personal therapy affect therapists' practice? *Journal of Counseling Psychology*, 46, 419–431.

MAIN, M. 1996. Introduction to the special section on attachment and psychopathology: Overview of the field of attachment. *Journal of Consulting and Clinical Psychology*, 64, 237–243.

MAIN, M., KAPLAN, N. & CASSIDY, J. 1985. Security in infancy, childhood, and adulthood: A move to the level of representation. *Monographs of the Society for Research in Child Development*, 50, 66–104.

MAIN, M. & WESTON, D. R. 1981. The quality of the toddler's relationship to mother and to father: Related to conflict behaviour and the readiness to establish new relationships. *Child Development*, 52, 932–940.

MARTIN, D. J., GARSKE, J. P. & DAVIS, M. K. 2000. Relation of the therapeutic alliance with outcome and other variables: A meta analytic review. *Journal of Consulting and Clinical Psychology*, 68, 438–450.

MASON, B. 2012. The personal and the professional: Core beliefs and the construction of bridges across difference. *In:* KRAUSE, I.-B. (ed.) *Culture and reflexivity in systemic psychotherapy: Mutual perspectives*. London: Karnac.

MASON, B., GIBNEY, P. & CRAGO, H. 2002. Family of origin work in training: Essential or dangerous? *Australian and New Zealand Journal of Family Therapy*, 23, 45–50.

MATAS, L., AREND, R. A. & SROUFE, A. 1978. Continuity of adaptation in the second year: The relationship between quality of attachment and later competence. *Child Development*, 49, 547–556.

MCCANDLESS, R. & EATOUGH, V. 2012. 'Her energy kind of went into a different place': A qualitative study examining supervisors' experience of promoting reflexive learning in students. *Journal of Marital and Family Therapy*, 38, 621–638, DOI: 10.1111/j.1752-0606.2011.00235.x.

MIKULINCER, M., GILLATH, O. & SHAVER, P. R. 2002. Activation of the attachment system in adulthood: Threat-related primes increase the accessibility of mental representations of attachment figures. *Journal of Personality and Social Psychology*, 83, 881–895.

MIKULINCER, M. & SHAVER, P. R. 2007. *Attachment in adulthood*. New York: Guilford Press.

MOHR, J. J., GELSO, C. J. & HILL, C. E. 2005. Client and counselor trainee attachment as predictors of session evaluation and countertransference behavior in first counseling sessions. *Journal of Counseling Psychology*, 52, 298–309.

MURPHY, R. A. & HALGIN, R. P. 1995. Influences on the career choice of psychotherapists. *Professional Psychology: Research and Practice*, 26, 422–426.

NAJAVITS, L. M. & STRUPP, H. H. 1994. Differences in the effectiveness of psychodynamic therapists: A process outcome study. *Psychotherapy*, 31.

NEL, P. W. 2006. Trainee perspectives on their family therapy training. *Journal of Family Therapy*, 28, 307–328.

NORCROSS, J. 2000. Psychotherapist self-care: Practitioner-tested, research informed strategies. *Professional Psychology: Research and Practice*, 31, 710–713.

NORCROSS, J. C. & GUY, J. D. 2007. *Leaving it at the office*. New York: Guilford Press.

NORCROSS, J. C., STRAUSSER-KIRTLAND, D. & MISSAR, C. D. 1988. The processes and outcomes of psychotherapists' personal treatment experiences. *Psychotherapy: Theory, Research, Practice, Training*, 25, 36–43.

ORCHOWSKI, L., EVANGELISTA, N. M. & PROBST, D. R. 2010. Enhancing supervisee reflectivity in clinical supervision: A case study illustration. *Psychotherapy Theory, Research,Practice, Training*, 47, 51–67.

PACK, M. 2013. Vicarious resilience: A multilayered model of stress and trauma. *Affilia*, 0886109913510088.

PAPELL, C. P. & SKOLNIK, L. 1992. The reflective practitioner: A contemporary paradigm's relevance for social work education. *Journal of Social Work Education*, 28, 18–26.

PARIS, E., LINVILLE, D. & ROSEN, K. 2006. Marriage and family therapists interns' experiences of growth. *Journal of Marital and Family Therapy*, 32, 45–57.

PEREIRA, T., LOCK, J. & OGGINS, J. 2006. Role of therapeutic alliance in family therapy for adolescent anorexia nervosa. *International Journal of Eating Disorders*, 39, 677–684.

PIETERSE, A. L., LEE, M., RITMEESTER, A. & COLLINS, N. M. 2013. Towards a model of self-awareness development for counselling and psychotherapy training. *Counselling Psychology Quarterly*, 26, 190–207.

PINSOF, W. M. & CATHERALL, D. R. 1986. The integrative psychotherapy alliance: Family, couple and individual therapy scales. *Journal of Marital and Family Therapy*, 12, 137–151.

RAIT, D. S. 2000. The therapeutic alliance in couples and family therapy. *Journal Clinical Psychology/In Session: Psychotherapy in Practice*, 56, 211–224.

RHODES, P., NGE, C., WALLIS, A. & HUNT, C. 2011. Learning and living systemic: Exploring the personal effects of family therapy training. *Contemporary Family Therapy*, 33, 335–347.

ROBBINS, M. S., LIIDLE, H. A., TURNER, C. W., DAKOF, G. A., ALEXANDER, J. F. & KOGAN, S. M. 2006. Adolescent and parent therapeutic alliances as predictors of dropout in multidimensional family therapy. *Journal of Family Psychology*, 20, 108–116.

ROSENBAUM, M. & RONEN, T. 1998. Clinical supervision from the standpoint of cognitive-behaviour therapy. *Psychotherapy*, 35, 220–230.

ROSENBLATT, P. C. 2009. Providing therapy can be therapeutic for a therapist. *American Journal of Psychotherapy*, 63, 169–181.

ROSSI, E. L. 2004. Stress-induced alternative gene splicing in mind-body medicine. *Advances in Mind Body Medicine*, 20, 12–19.

RUCH, G. 2002. From triangle to spiral: Reflective practice in social work education, practice and research. *Social Work Education*, 21, 199–216.

SABLE, P. 2004. Attachment, ethology and adult psychotherapy. *Attachment & Human Development*, 6, 3–19.

SAFRAN, J. D. & MURAN, J. C. 2000. *Negotiating the therapeutic alliance: A relational treatment guide*. New York: Guilford Press.

SANDS, A. 2000. *Falling for therapy: Psychotherapy from a client's point of view.* Houndmills: Macmillan Press Ltd.

SAUER, E. M., LOPEZ, F., G. & GORMLEY, B. 2003. Respective contributions of therapist and client adult attachment orientations to the development of the early working alliance: A preliminary growth modeling study. *Psychotherapy Research*, 13, 371–382.

SAVIC-JABROW, P. C. 2010. Where do counsellors in private practice receive their support? A pilot study. *Counselling and Psychotherapy Research*, 10, 229–232.

SCHON, D. A. 1991. *The reflective practitioner: How professionals think in action.* London: Ashgate.

SCHORE, A. N. 2005. Attachment, affect regulation, and the developing right brain: Linking developmental neuroscience to pediatrics. *Pediatrics in Review*, 26, 204–211.

SCHORE, J. R. & SCHORE, A. N. 2008. Modern attachment theory: The central role of affect regulation in development and treatment. *Clinical Social Work Journal*, 36, 9–20.

SHILKRET, C. J. 2005. Some clinical applications of attachment theory in adult psychotherapy. *Clinical Social Work Journal*, 33, 55–68.

SILVERMAN, D. 2010. *Interpreting qualitative data.* London: Sage Publications Ltd.

SLADE, A. 1999. Attachment theory and research. *In:* CASSIDY, J. & SHAVER, P. R. (eds.) *Handbook of attachment: Theory, research and application.* New York: Guilford Press.

STEELE, H. & STEELE, M. 2005. Understanding and resolving emotional conflict. *In:* GROSSMANN, K. E., GROSSMAN, K. & WATERS, E. (eds.) *Attachment from infancy to adulthood: The major longitudinal studies.* New York: Guilford Press.

STEELE, H., STEELE, M. & FONAGY, P. 1996. Associations among attachment classifications of mothers, fathers, and their infants. *Child Development*, 67, 541–555.

STRATTON, P. & HANKS, H. 2016. PPD as processes of learning that enable the practitioner to create a self that is equipped for higher levels of professional mastery. *In:* VETERE, A. & STRATTON, P. (eds.) *Interacting selves.* Oxon: Routledge.

STREET, E. & RIVETT, M. 1996. Stress and coping in the practice of family therapy: A British survey. *Journal of Family Therapy*, 18, 303–319.

THOMAS, R. A. 1999. Early attachment and later development. *In:* CASSIDY, J. & SHAVER, P. R. (eds.) *Handbook of attachment: Theory, research, and clinical applications.* New York: Guilford Press.

THOMPSON, S. & THOMPSON, N. 2008. *The critically reflective practitioner.* London: Palgrave Macmillan.

TOTSUKA, Y. 2014. 'Which aspects of social GGRRAAACCEEESSS grab you most?' The social GGRRAAACCEEESSS exercise for a supervision group to promote therapists' self-reflexivity. *Journal of Family Therapy,* (Online First) doi: 10.1111/1467-6427.12026.

VAN IJZENDOORN, M. H. 1995. Adult attachment representations, parental responsiveness, and infant attachment: A meta-analysis on the predictive validity of the adult attachment interview. *Psychological Bulletin,* 117, 387–403.

VANDENBERGHE, L. & MARTINS DA SILVEIRA, J. 2013. Therapist self-as-context and the curative relationship. *Journal of Contemporary Psychotherapy,* 43, 159–167.

VANDENBERGHE, L., PRADO, F. C. & DE CAMARGO, E. A. 2012. Spirituality and religion in psychotherapy: Views of Brazilian psychotherapists. *International Perspectives in Psychology: Research, Practice, Consultation,* 1, 79–93.

VETERE, A. & DALLOS, R. 2008. Systemic therapy and attachment narratives. *Journal of Family Therapy,* 30, 374–385.

WALLIN, D. J. 2007. *Attachment in psychotherapy.* New York: Guilford Press.

WALSH, R. 2011. Lifestyle and mental health. *American Psychologist,* 1–14.

WARD, A. 2010. The use of self in relationship-based practice. *In:* RUCH, G., TURNEY, D. & WARD, A. (eds.) *Relationship based social work.* London: Jessica Kingsley Publisher.

WATERS, E., MERRICK, S., TREBOUX, D., CROWELL, J. & ALBERSHEIM, L. 2000. Attachment security in infancy and early adulthood: A twenty-year longitudinal study. *Child Development,* 71, 684–689.

WHEELER, S. & ELLIOT, R. 2008. What do counsellors and psychotherapists need to know about research? *Counselling and Psychotherapy Research,* 8, 133–135.

WILLIAMS, B., CARPENTER, J. & TIMMS, J. 2015. Family and systemic psychotherapists' experiences of personal therapeutic consultations as a tool for personal and professional development in training. *Journal of Family Therapy,* 37, 563–582.

WILLIAMS, E. N., POLSTER, D., GRIZZARD, M. B., ROCKENBAUGH, J. & JUDGE, A. B. 2003. What happens when therapists feel bored or anxious? A qualitative study of distracting self-awareness and therapists' management strategies. *Journal of Contemporary Psychotherapy,* 33.

WITTENBORN, A. K. 2012. Exploring the influence of the attachment organizations of novice therapists on their delivery of emotionally focused therapy for couples. *Journal of Marital and Family Therapy,* 38, 50–62.

YOO, H., BARTLE-HARING, S. & GANGAMMA, R. 2016. Predicting premature termination with alliance at sessions 1 and 3: An exploratory study. *Journal of Family Therapy*, 38, 5–17.

YUSOF, Y. 2005. Penilaian kesihatan mental dan kerja sosial. *In:* HILLALUDDIN, A. H., AHMAD RAMLY, F. Z., SAYUTI, R. & YUSOF, Y. (eds.) *Polisi, perundangan dan amalan kerja sosial.* Sintok, Kedah: Penerbit Universiti Utara Malaysia.

YUSOF, Y. (2012a). Therapist attachment styles and therapeutic alliance in family therapy (Unpublished doctoral dissertation). (PhD), University of Bristol, Bristol.

YUSOF, Y. (2012b, 4–7 November). Interviewing the experts: A reflexive cross-cultural experience. Paper presented at the First UUM COB Qualitative Research Conference, 784–789, Kuala Lumpur. ISBN 978-983-44592-4-6.

YUSOF, Y. & CARPENTER, J. S. W. 2012. A survey of family therapists' adult attachment styles in the United Kingdom. *Contemporary Family Therapy*, 34, 443–592.

YUSOF, Y. & CARPENTER, J. S. W. 2014. The impact of family therapists' adult attachment styles on their career choice and approach to therapy: An interpretive phenomenological analysis. *Journal of Social Work Practice: Psychotherapeutic Approaches in Health, Welfare and the Community.*

YUSOF, Y. & CARPENTER, J. S. W. 2016. Therapists' attachment styles and therapeutic alliance. *Journal of Family Therapy*, 38, 59–81.

ZAYAS, V., MISCHEL, W., SHODA, Y. & ABER, L.J. (2011). Roots of adult attachment: maternal caregiving at 18 months predicts adult peer and partner relationship. *Social Psychological and Personality Science*, 2(3), 289–297.

ZERUBAVEL, N. & WRIGHT, M. O. D. 2012. The dilemma of the wounded healer. *Psychotherapy*, 49, 482–491.

Index

www.ingramcontent.com/pod-product-compliance
Ingram Content Group UK Ltd.
Pitfield, Milton Keynes, MK11 3LW, UK
UKHW021032150926
475561UK00003B/68

9 781352 007329